MW00588291

BIBLICAL STUDIES FROM THE CATHOLIC BIBLICAL ASSOCIATION OF AMERICA

GENERAL EDITOR

FRANK J. MATERA

EDITORIAL BOARD

Previous Volumes in Biblical Studies from the CBA

1. *A Concise Theology of the New Testament* • Frank J. Matera

2. *Letters to the Johannine Circle: 1–3 John* • Francis J. Moloney, SDB

THE LANDSCAPE OF THE GOSPELS

A DEEPER MEANING

DONALD SENIOR, CP

Biblical Studies
from the Catholic Biblical
Association
No. 3

Paulist Press
New York Mahwah, NJ

Cover image by sakkmesterke/ Shutterstock.com
Cover design by Dawn Massa, Lightly Salted Graphics
Book design by Lynn Else

Library of Congress Cataloging-in-Publication Data
Names: Senior, Donald, author.
Title: The landscape of the Gospels : a deeper meaning / Donald Senior, C.P.
Description: New York / Mahwah, NJ : Paulist Press, 2020. | Series: Biblical studies from the Catholic Biblical Association of America | Includes bibliographical references. | Summary: "The Landscape of the Gospels explores the geography of the gospel narratives and the Acts of the Apostles and reveals the deeper meaning that this often overlooked dimension gives the biblical texts" — Provided by publisher.
Identifiers: LCCN 2019056859 (print) | LCCN 2019056860 (ebook) | ISBN 9780809154357 (paperback) | ISBN 9781587688300 (ebook)
Subjects: LCSH: Bible. Gospels—Geography. | Palestine—Geography. | Bible. Gospels—Criticism, interpretation, etc. | Bible. Acts—Geography. | Bible. Acts—Criticism, interpretation, etc. | Bible. Gospels—History of Biblical events. | Bible. Acts—History of Biblical events.
Classification: LCC BS2555.6.P43 S46 2020 (print) | LCC BS2555.6.P43 (ebook) | DDC 226/.091—dc23
LC record available at https://lccn.loc.gov/2019056859
LC ebook record available at https://lccn.loc.gov/2019056860

ISBN 978-0-8091-5435-7 (paperback)
ISBN 978-1-58768-830-0 (e-book)

Published by Paulist Press
997 Macarthur Boulevard
Mahwah, NJ 07430
www.paulistpress.com

Printed and bound in the
United States of America

Contents

Map Index vi

About the Series vii

Introduction: The Biblical Landscape 1

Chapter One: The Landscape of the
    Gospel of Mark 24

Chapter Two: The Landscape of the
    Gospel of Matthew 49

Chapter Three: The Landscape of the
    Gospel of Luke and the Acts of the Apostles 63

Chapter Four: The Landscape of the
    Gospel of John 97

Conclusion: Seeking the Holy Land 121

Notes 127

Select Bibliography 133

Map Index

Map 1: Middle East from Egypt to Mesopotamia 6

Map 2: Topography of Israel.. 9

Map 3: Galilee 11

Map 4: Samaria with Judea.. 15

Map 5: Israel with the Negev 18

Map 6: Israel in the Time of Jesus 36

Map 7: Jerusalem Vicinity 39

Map 8: Judea with Egypt.. 52

Map 9: Galilee with Former Northern Tribes............................... 55

Map 10: Jerusalem Temple Built by Herod the Great 65

Map 11: Jerusalem and Bethany at the Time of Jesus 73

Map 12: Judea and Samaria 80

Map 13: Missionary Journeys of Paul 83

Map 14: Final Journey of Paul to Rome 91

Map 15: Baptismal Site at the Jordan River 102

Map 16: Journey through Samaria.. 108

Map 17: Jerusalem at the Time of Jesus... 111

About the Series

This series, Biblical Studies from the Catholic Biblical Association of America, seeks to bridge the gap between the technical exegetical work of the academic community and the educational and pastoral needs of the ecclesial community. Combining careful exegesis with a theological understanding of the text, the members of the Catholic Biblical Association of America have written these volumes in a style that is accessible to an educated, nonspecialized audience, without compromising academic integrity.

These volumes deal with biblical texts and themes that are important and vital for the life and ministry of the Church. While some focus on specific biblical books or particular texts, others are concerned with important theological themes, still others with archaeological and geographical issues, and still others with questions of interpretation. Through this series, the members of the Catholic Biblical Association of America are eager to present the results of their research in a way that is relevant to an interested audience that goes beyond the confines of the academic community.

The Biblical Landscape

My first visit to the Holy Land took place in 1968, traveling on an archaeological tour with a group of fellow students from the University of Louvain in Belgium, where I was pursuing doctoral studies in New Testament. The professor who was directing my doctoral work, the late Frans Neirynck, was an eminent scholar whose profound knowledge of the Bible and of the scholarly literature interpreting it was legendary. However, when I told him I was going to visit archaeological sites in Israel and Jordan, he was unenthusiastic and wondered what I could learn there that I could not discover in the university's library. In fact, I would later learn that my beloved and highly respected mentor would visit the Holy Land only once in his life, and that for a brief time to attend an international conference held in Jerusalem on the Synoptic Problem!

Professor Neirynck was admittedly correct, to the extent that virtually everything in that region today is different from the first-century region that shaped the New Testament. Many among the present-day Israeli population are very Western and modern, even as they find meaning in their roots in the Jewish people of ancient Israel. The Palestinians, a native people who in many ways derive from a mix of the various peoples who have populated this region over the centuries, currently have a culture, architecture, history, and religious loyalties different from their first-century ancestors. The distinctive features of today's traditional Palestinian cultures—in dress, food, architecture, and so on—remind

1

visitors from the West that they are stepping into something — for them — of an exotic culture and thus evoke the biblical world. But, in fact, the world of the contemporary Middle East is vastly different from the world of the first century.

THE CONSTANT OF THE LAND

The one exception to this discontinuity is the land. The land, too, has altered somewhat in the course of history due to such factors as climate change, different patterns of forestation and agriculture, and the impact of human habitation and industry on the land. Yet the overall contours of the land — its mountains and seas and rivers, its desert boundaries, its basic climate — remain substantially the same. Not only that, but the retentive historical memory of generations of people there and the work of modern archaeology have enabled us to relate the events and locations of the Gospels, for example, to the current biblical landscape. Alert travelers to the region encounter a real connection to a fundamental dimension of the biblical texts, namely its geographical context or its "landscape" understood in a broad sense. And those who are biblically literate can associate certain locations and features of the land with the biblical story of ancient Israel: the Israelites crossing the Sinai Peninsula; Moses gazing at the promised land from the heights of Mount Nebo in the Transjordan; Joshua leading the people across the Jordan River and invading Jericho; cities and places laden with biblical memories such as Jerusalem and Bethlehem, Nazareth, Capernaum, and the Sea of Galilee.[1] While a modern observer can glean a lot from photos, videos, and literature on the subject, there is something compelling — and valuable — about experiencing the land of the Bible firsthand.

All human beings and all human history are profoundly influenced by the land on which we stand. In a most fundamental way, we belong to the earth and our identity is shaped by it. We can think of the notion of "land" or geography in a variety of ways. Land can be defined geologically by the physical make-up of a particular region, including its contours, its climate, its mineral content, and its relationship to the surrounding areas. From this vantage point, land or landscape is made up of mountains, valleys, plains, rivers, the sea, the desert, urban and rural areas, and so on.

But the land or landscape is also entwined with the *history* that has played out in the arena of a particular location. Often the lay of the land will dictate how some major events or trends over time happen. The landscape of an area sets the stage for the history that plays out on its surface. Resources such as an adequate water supply and climate enable agriculture. Proximity to traversable canyons and mountain passes encourage trade and commerce. Natural features such as high ground and visibility offer protection in times of threat. From time immemorial these are the conditions that dictated the location of villages and cities and help set the context for the flow of history. And, reciprocally, human events or human artifacts can help shape the land itself; for example, the construction of a city or a port or the laying out of a trade route can change the physical character of a location and add new layers of meaning.

Drawing on all these levels, a specific landscape can take on, over time, a symbolic meaning, what some modern interpreters have referred to as the "spiritual landscape." The history of a people and some of the defining moments in that history (a battle, an exile, the influence of a singular personage or ruler, etc.) leave their imprint on the land and contribute to its symbolic meaning.

THE GOSPELS AND THE LAND

Understandably, most Christians read the Four Gospels for their portrayal of Jesus and his mission and find there a vision of human life before God that is beautiful and compelling. The Acts of the Apostles—the second volume Luke appended to his

Gospel — illustrates the rapid and miraculous spread of the gospel message out into the Mediterranean world and illustrates the essential missionary nature of the church. In most instances, therefore, interpreters of the Gospels focus on the words and deeds of Jesus as the privileged source to construct our understanding of the profound identity of Jesus and the mission of the community founded in his name. But the Gospels, we know, are not theological treatises or first-century theological discourses. They are, rather, narratives, stories rooted in a particular time and place. Even though the composition of the four Gospels took place over time and may not have been set in writing until forty or more years after the events they portray, the context of Jesus's life and mission they depict is set in the first third of first-century Palestine. And it is evident that the Gospels do not simply record Jesus's sayings and describe his actions, but have set their narrative in a varied landscape, a landscape that in many instances is drenched in a long history of biblical events preceding the time of Jesus and carrying meaning from those past events.

To take obvious examples, when Jesus is plunged into the Jordan River and then thrust into the desert in the opening scenes of Mark's Gospel, these are not simply "neutral" geographical locations but "spiritual landscapes" that evoke the origin of Israel and its entrance into the promised land as portrayed in the Bible. Likewise, Jesus's dramatic entry into the Jerusalem temple is hardly the visit of an observer curious about a large human structure but a moment when the Son of God enters the house of his Father, an arena drenched in biblical history and with multiple layers of meaning. When the Acts of the Apostles describes Paul crossing over for the first time into Europe as in his first visit to Philippi (Acts 16:6–12), or arriving in Rome, the imperial capital, at the climax of the narrative (Acts 28:11–31), the geographical and historical contexts of these locations add new levels of meaning.

The thesis of this study is that we can savor more of the meaning of the Gospel narratives and of the Acts of the Apostles if we keep an eye on their "landscape," that is, on their geographical layout and the biblical history intimately related to this geography. Some of the settings described in the Gospels may simply be the narrative backdrop of the account: for example, Jesus enters a house or sits in a boat or travels to the surrounding villages. So we should be leery of ascribing symbolic meaning to every detail of the Gospel narratives. But in many instances, the evangelists and the traditions they are drawing on intend to evoke a deeper, symbolic meaning to the places in which the gospel drama unfolds. That symbolic meaning may be entwined with macroareas or regions such as "Galilee" or "Judea" or "Samaria" where Israel's history as portrayed in the Old Testament Scriptures leaves an overlay of meaning. Or it can extend to aspects of the land that evoke universal iconic meanings such as mountains, deserts, or the sea—each of which have significant roles in the story of Jesus. And a symbolic meaning can be entwined with a very particular location: the city of Jerusalem and its temple; Caesarea Philippi or Caesarea Maritima; Bethlehem or Bethany.

THE LAY OF THE LAND

Most events depicted in the Bible took place in a relatively small geographical arena some 350 miles long and little more than 60 miles wide, roughly the size of New Jersey.[2] Ancient Israel was a strip of territory that formed the land bridge between two regions of major powers in the ancient world. It was a part of the so-called Fertile Crescent, the crescent-shaped land mass that included the region of Mesopotamia to the northeast between the Tigris and Euphrates rivers, the location of successive dominant civilizations such as Assyria, Babylon, and Persia; and to the southwest stood Egypt, an enduring ancient civilization that dominated the history of the region for centuries. Like Mesopotamia, Egypt, too, was blessed with a major water system, the Nile River, that ran the length of its territory and fed its development of agriculture and

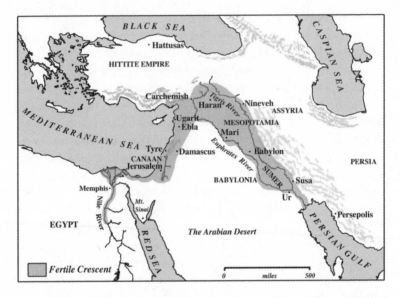

commerce, enabling it to achieve its powerful status far in advance of most other regions.

The strip of land where the biblical saga would unfold stood between these two powerful regions and much of its history would be shaped by this geographical location. Along the Mediterranean coast of the region would run the Via Maris (the "Way of the Sea"), the ancient trade route that connected Egypt with its competing powerful partners in Mesopotamia. In subsequent eras, conquering armies such as the Assyrians, the Babylonians, the Greeks under Alexander the Great, the Romans, the Arab conquerors, the Crusaders, the Ottomans, and the Allied powers of World War I would traverse that same route to impose their hegemony on the region.

Today that land bridge is occupied by the modern states of Israel, Palestine, Jordan, and parts of Syria and Lebanon. And the political and economic environment of the region continue to be influenced by its strategic location and its past history. Even the choice of name for this region today has inevitable political overtones. The term *Palestine*, for example, was first designated by the Roman Emperor Hadrian in the period after the second Jewish revolt against Rome (AD 132) and was intended to impose on the provinces of Judea and Syria a name derived from the "Philistines," the traditional enemies of ancient Israel. For Palestinians today, however, the designation "Palestine" reflects their aspirations for a state of their own. At the same time, the modern State of Israel lays claim to the name and territory of ancient Israel described in the Bible. The land claims of both these populations have fueled the unresolved conflict between Israelis and the Palestinians and stoked wider tensions in the region. Perhaps the safest term is to refer to the region as the *Holy Land*, although this name, too, is derived from a religious perspective that not all would share.

THE LANDSCAPE OF THE GOSPELS

Although a relatively small tract of land, the Holy Land is marked by striking geographical diversity, including a Mediterranean coastal region running the length of the area on the west, a significant body of fresh water in the Sea of Galilee in the north, the important Jordan River cleaving the center of the region, a small stretch of the Red Sea in the south, mountainous regions in its northern and central areas enveloping alluvial valleys in its central highlands, and desert regions to its south and east, including the dominant presence of the Rift or Jordan valley slicing the country from north to south and, at its lowest level, forming the Dead Sea. To describe the span of the country, multiple biblical passages speak of the land stretching from "Dan to Beersheba," that is from the northernmost boundary in Upper Galilee to the southern boundary of the Negev (see, e.g., Judg 20:1; 1 Sam 3:20; 2 Sam 3:10; 17:11; 24:2; 25:15; 1 Kgs 5:5).

Within this broader geographical framework of the Bible, the events of Jesus's life portrayed in the Gospels are even more confined. There are some breakouts from this narrower geographical focus: for example, in Matthew's Gospel, the flight of the Holy Family to find refuge in Egypt; and, especially for Mark, the incursion of Jesus into the Gentile territories of Tyre and Sidon in present-day Lebanon, and the Decapolis, a region on the eastern side of the Sea of Galilee. Predicted at the conclusion of Luke's Gospel and explicitly narrated in the Acts of the Apostles, the gospel landscape explodes out into the Mediterranean world, even to Rome itself, an outreach only "promised" in Matthew or hinted at in Mark and John. If one takes into account the Prologue of John's Gospel, the "landscape" of Jesus's mission becomes "spatial" beginning in the very life of God and descends through the cosmos to "become flesh."

But for the most part the gospel landscape is confined to five major areas: Galilee, the Sea of Galilee and the Jordan Valley, Samaria, the desert, and Judea and Jerusalem.

GALILEE

The northern region of the Holy Land is Galilee, a name possibly derived from the Hebrew that means simply the "district." This is the arena in which most of Jesus's public ministry was located, particularly, as we will see, in the Synoptic Gospels, less so in the Gospel of John. Galilee itself contains two distinct geographical regions. Running across the northern limits of this region at the current Lebanese and Syrian border is a mountain range in an area designated as "Upper Galilee"—not simply because it is to the north but because of its elevation (3,000 ft.). Dominating the horizon of Upper Galilee are the heights of Mount Meron and farther to the east the tallest of all mountains in the area, Mount Hermon, frequently cited in the Psalms for the beauty of its snow-capped peak. Jesus and his disciples visited this area in the region of Caesarea Philippi, present-day Banias, the area in which the headwaters of the Jordan River emerge from the Mount Hermon range.

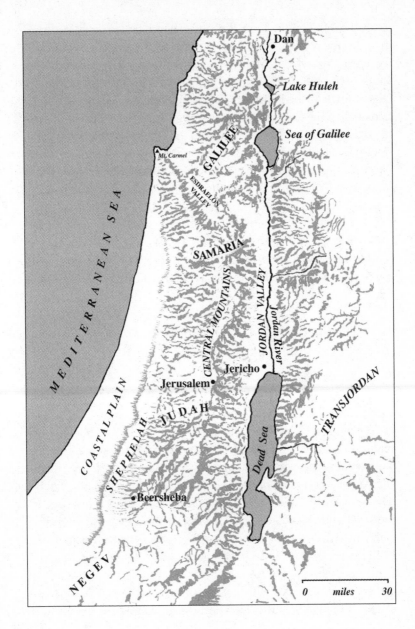

"Lower Galilee," on the other hand, is less elevated and includes the relatively flat land that stretches from the Sea of Galilee west toward the Mediterranean coastal plain. Immediately south of present-day Haifa and its harbor begins the Jezreel Valley (also known as the Plains of Esdrelon), with its western point nestled against the Carmel mountain range and stretching east across the entire region of Lower Galilee to the Rift or Jordan Valley. This is a richly fertile region and has been the breadbasket of the Holy Land and an attractive target of its enemies from ancient times (the name *Jezreel* itself is from the Hebrew meaning "God sows"). Nazareth is located in this region and the Gospels note other places in Lower Galilee where Jesus preached and healed, such as Naim and Cana. In the Synoptic Gospels, Jesus also crosses the border near the Mediterranean coast of Upper Galilee and visits the region of Tyre and Sidon, ancient cities located in present-day Lebanon.

The Historical and Symbolic Character of the Galilean Landscape

History also gives this region a certain personality. In the eight century BC, the Assyrian Empire had expanded to the west and crushed the Northern Kingdom of Israel, inaugurating a form of "ethnic cleansing" — moving large segments of the Israelite population into forced exile and introducing foreign people into the land, turning the North ultimately into an Assyrian province. Later, Alexander's conquest of the entire region in the third century BC left a veneer of Hellenistic culture across the land. This appears to have been particularly true in some of the regions surrounding Galilee, such as the Decapolis, or league of ten cities, established in the wake of Alexander's conquest. These largely Gentile and Hellenistic cities were found on the eastern shore of the Sea of Galilee, although Bet Shean, a major city to the south and west of the Sea of Galilee, was also part of this league. To the north in

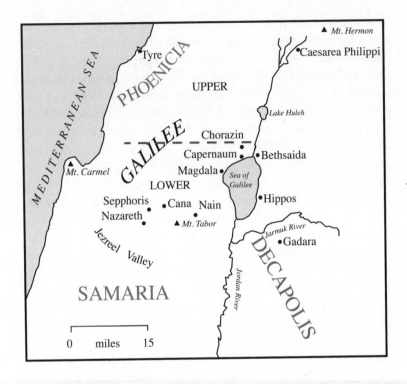

the region of Caesarea Philippi and to the northwest toward the area of Tyre and Sidon, were also Gentile regions. The traditional trade route of the Via Maris, which ran across the Sinai Peninsula from Egypt and then north along the Mediterranean coast until turning east through the Carmel range, then across Lower Galilee itself and on to Damascus and beyond, no doubt contributed to the spread of foreign commerce and influence in the region. The dominant language of the region in the first century was Aramaic, but inscriptions have also been found in Greek and it is possible many in the region would have been bilingual.

Although Jewish populations remained in the area, the Galilee region was not fully incorporated under Jewish rule until the time of the Hasmonean dynasty, which extended its hegemony into the region little more than a century before the birth of Jesus. Later, with the reign of the Herodians at the beginning of the first century, Roman influence would be felt.[3] During the lifetime of Jesus in Galilee, the ruler was Herod the Great's son, Herod Antipas (3 BC to AD 39). Antipas's reign as a vassal of the empire shielded Galilee from direct Roman occupation, but the imperial influence was clear. Only after AD 41 and the death of Antipas's successor Herod Agrippa did Romans directly rule Galilee. During Jesus's years as a young adult, Antipas had constructed two major cities in honor of the emperor, Sepphoris to the west, only four miles from Nazareth, and Tiberias on the western shore of the Sea of Galilee. Over time these urban populations changed the economic equilibrium of Galilee, absorbing a substantial amount of the produce from the small subsistent farms in the region. Although Nazareth is close to Sepphoris and Capernaum is near Tiberias, there is no mention in the Gospels of Jesus ever visiting either of these urban centers. Some have speculated that Joseph, a craftsman or carpenter, moved to Nazareth to be near the building projects at Sepphoris and perhaps that Jesus himself would have also been involved there.

These incursions of Greco-Roman culture into the region of Galilee, as well as its past history as part of the defeated and scattered Northern Kingdom, made Galilee something of an outlier from the viewpoint of Judea and its capital Jerusalem, which viewed itself as the center of Jewish orthodoxy. Nathaniel's question in the opening chapter of John's Gospel captures the mood: "Can anything good come from Nazareth?" (John 1:46).

At the same time, modern archaeology has confirmed that the region was strongly Jewish in its culture and religion. Although a veneer of Hellenistic influence can be found, especially in the cities and in the homes of the elite, such as mosaics, the layout of city grids, and such cultural markers as public baths, theaters, and hippodromes, there is also evidence of Jewish presence and religious observance, with ritual purification baths, or *mikvot*, built into houses, the presence of stone vessels used to observe dietary laws, and an absence of pork bones. In the last several decades archaeologists have also discovered the remains of what appeared to be several first-century synagogues in the Galilee region, another indicator of the vibrancy of Jewish life in the region.[4] Synagogues in this period were quasi-public buildings, serving as a place for formal daily prayers, as well as a kind of town hall or meeting place for key events and discussions. Later, they would take on their own distinctive architecture. The Gospels make clear that Jesus used the Galilean synagogues as an important arena for his own teaching and healing activity.

THE SEA OF GALILEE AND THE JORDAN VALLEY

Beginning at the current Lebanese border and at the site of the ancient city of Dan, the headwaters of the Jordan River emerge, draining the winter snows of the Mount Hermon range. At first a mountain stream, the Jordan picks up momentum as it descends into the Sea of Galilee, the body of water some twelve miles long and six miles wide, located at six hundred feet below sea level, that dominates the region and figures so prominently in the Gospels. In the Synoptic Gospels, the first disciples of Jesus are fishermen on the Sea of Galilee. The sea was well stocked with fish and there is evidence from the time of Jesus that salted fish from the region was exported throughout the empire. The alternate name of the seaside fishing village of Magdala was Tarichaeae, referring to the wooden structures or "towers" used to dry salted fish. The Gospels themselves testify to the thriving fishing industry of first-century Galilee. Archaeology has also shown that the Galilee region produced its own distinctive ceramics. Some of the most haunting scenes revealing Jesus's transcendent identity take place on the Sea. On the eastern shore of the Sea was the "Decapolis" region, a league of ten mainly Gentile towns.[5] Jesus's foray into this area is a harbinger of the Gentile mission yet to come.

The Jordan River reemerges from the southern end of this body of fresh water and begins its increasing descent, cutting through the Jordan Valley and finally south of Jericho, emptying into the Dead Sea. The entire Jordan Valley is part of the great "Rift," a remarkable geological feature of this land that cuts deep into the surface of the earth and stretches from its origin north beyond Lebanon, moves down through all of the Holy Land, and continues along the Red Sea and the Sinai Peninsula until it ends in East Africa at Lake Victoria. In the brackish waters of the Dead Sea, the Rift reaches the lowest point on the surface of the earth. The stretch of arid land between the southern tip of the Dead Sea and the northern edge of the Red Sea, located at the current twin cities of Aqaba (Jordan) and Eilat (Israel), is what the Bible calls the "Arava" or "dry land," a trackless wasteland that merges with the Negev and forms the southern belt of desert that envelops all of the Holy Land to its south.

While much of the Jordan Valley is arid, the soil on the eastern bank of the Jordan between the Sea of Galilee and Jericho is rich farmland. Unlike the western bank of the Jordan, in the current State of Israel, which is deeply rutted by erosion and has less flat surface, the eastern bank is more level and is well suited to agriculture, although it depends currently on water from the Jordan River and from water channeled from Syria. At the time of Jesus, for example, those traveling from Galilee to Jerusalem down the Jordan Valley route would normally move down the eastern side of the Jordan, thereby avoiding any contact with hostile Samaria and finding travel on foot or by animal and carriage easier to navigate on the level land.

SAMARIA

Samaria is the mountainous region that lies between Galilee to the north and Judea to the south. The estrangement between Samaritans and Jews has deep historical roots. Originally it was

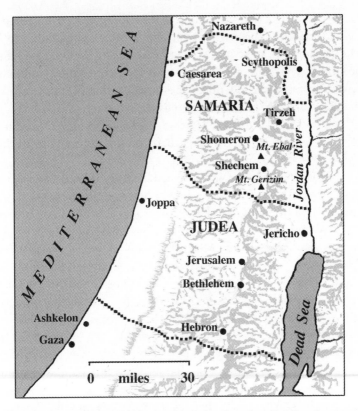

part of the northern kingdom of Israel after the division between Judah and the Northern tribes during the reign of Solomon's successors. Around 884 BC, King Omri moved the capital of the North from Tirzeh to the city of Shomeron—the probable etymology of the word *Samaritan*. The entire region fell to the Assyrian invasion in the eighth century. The Samaritans themselves trace their religious ancestry to the original tribes of Ephraim and Manasseh and claim to preserve the original Mosaic religion. Later, in the wake of the sixth-century Babylonian exile, the returning Judean exiles accused the Samaritans and their religion of being corrupted by foreign influences and did not permit Samaritans to participate in the reconstruction of Jerusalem and its temple. The Samaritans themselves constructed their own temple on the holy site of Mount Gerizim, near modern-day Nablus, or ancient Shechem, around 550 BC and conducted what they considered authentic Jewish worship there. Under the short-lived Jewish monarchy of the Hasmonean dynasty, the Samaritan temple was destroyed in 110 BC by John Hyrcanus. The Samaritans continued to worship at this site, and a modern Samaritan community remains in this area until today.

This long-term tension between the Jews and the Samaritans is reflected in several New Testament passages. In the mission discourse of Matthew's Gospel, Jesus instructs his disciples to restrict their mission to Israel and "not [to] go into pagan territory or enter a Samaritan town" (Matt 10:5), viewing both "pagans" and "Samaritans" as nearly equivalent and definitely outside of the realm of God's people. In Luke's Gospel, Jesus tells the parable of the Good Samaritan (Luke 10:29–37) who cares for the wounds of a man attacked and left abandoned. And Jesus laments that the only leper to return and give thanks, among the group of ten he had cured, was a Samaritan (Luke 17:16). Both passages bank on Jesus's audience's assumption that Jews would be more virtuous than Samaritans. At the beginning of Jesus's journey to Jerusalem, Luke's Gospel uniquely cites the fact that Samaritan villages "would not welcome him because the destination of his journey was Jerusalem" (9:52–53). When the disciples want to "call down fire from heaven to consume them" (9:54), Jesus rebukes them and continues on his way.

In the Acts of the Apostles, however, Luke describes at some length an early mission to Samaria that had very positive results. After the persecution triggered by Steven's martyrdom, some of the Jerusalem Christians take refuge in Samaria and begin to preach the gospel there (Acts 8:1, 4). Later, the apostle Philip goes to Samaria and "proclaim[s] the Messiah to them" (Acts 8:5); the Samaritans respond enthusiastically and many of the sick and possessed were healed. Luke notes that "there was great joy in that city" (8:8). When the apostles in Jerusalem hear this good news about the Samaritans, they send Peter and John there to confer on them the Holy Spirit (8:14–17). Luke also recounts the strange incident in Samaria about "Simon the Magician," who was impressed with the power of the apostles and its impact, and offers to purchase some of their power (Acts 8:9–24). When rebuked by Peter, Simon repents. The narrative about the mission to Samaria ends on a jubilant note: "So when they [the apostles] had testified and preached the word of the Lord, they returned to Jerusalem and preached the good news to many Samaritan villages" (Acts 8:25).

And, of course, the Gospel of John uniquely describes the encounter of Jesus with a Samaritan woman at the well, leading to the belief of the Samaritans in Jesus as the Savior of the world (John 4:1–42).[6]

THE DESERT

The biblical arena is bounded on its east and south by desert regions. Moving east from Jerusalem, the land abruptly descends into the Jordan Valley; the sparse rainfall in this region creates the Judean desert, or as it is also called, the Judean wilderness. This arid and deeply rutted region spreads east to the Dead Sea and into the TransJordan. Here the Jordan River meets the brackish Dead Sea, the lowest place on the surface of the earth, and here is located the oasis city of Jericho (which claims to be the oldest inhabited city on earth!). The Four Gospels, each in their own way, locate the beginning of Jesus's own ministry here, in his encounter with the desert prophet John the Baptist. John's Gospel seems to locate the baptismal activity of John on the eastern side of the Jordan River, a desert region now in present-day Jordan.

Another enormous strip of desert, called the "Negev" (in Hebrew meaning "dry"), runs across the entire southern boundary of Israel and makes up more than 50 percent of its landmass.

THE LANDSCAPE OF THE GOSPELS

The ancient city of Hebron stands near the edge of this desert area that descends into the Negev, and the city of Beersheba, associated with Abraham and stories of the patriarchs, is located in the heart of this desert region. The Gospels do not place any accounts of Jesus's activity in this region, although the Acts of the Apostles describes the deacon Philip encountering the Ethiopian eunuch who is returning home through Gaza, the desert strip that separates Israel from Egypt (see Acts 8:26–40). For the Bible as a whole, the defining exodus event brings the Israelites from their slavery in Egypt across the Sinai Peninsula. Their hesitations and doubts lead to a forty-year desert sojourn in the Sinai Peninsula and in the Negev Region, before they travel up the eastern side of the Rift Valley and, under the leadership of Joshua, cross the Jordan to take possession of the Land. This biblical drama forms the backdrop to the inauguration of Jesus's own mission and its desert setting.

JUDEA AND JERUSALEM

The southern region of Judea and its capital Jerusalem form the other end of the geographical axis of the gospel drama that stretches from Galilee to Jerusalem. Bethlehem, the ancestral city of David and the place of Jesus's birth; and on the eastern slope of the Mount of Olives, Bethany, a place of respite for Jesus in the home of Mary, Martha, and Lazarus; and, most of all, Jerusalem itself and its temple, are the location of the most dramatic and decisive events of Jesus's life and mission. This region stands astride the central mountain range and is bounded on the east by the Jordan, or Rift, Valley and on the west by the Mediterranean Coastal plain. The Bible notes that David captured Jerusalem from the Jebusite tribe (2 Sam 5:6–10). Shrewdly, he made it the new central capital of his kingdom, establishing there his royal palace and bringing to the city the ark of the covenant—thereby fusing in Jerusalem the political and religious center of Israel, a role it continued to play for most of Israel's history.

Over time, the temple of Jerusalem would eclipse all local shrines and consolidate all of the cult of Israel. The priestly caste that served the temple would thereby make Jerusalem not only the seat of government but the bastion of religious orthodoxy. The temple built by David's son and successor, Solomon, would undergo various iterations in step with the fate of Israel. The chaotic demise of the Hasmonean dynasty and its ultimate replacement by Herod the Great around 36 BC set the stage for the expansion and radical renovation of the Jerusalem temple, the temple that would become an arena for Jesus's prophetic teaching in the Gospels and trigger the events leading to his crucifixion. By the time of Jesus's entry into Jerusalem during his public ministry, the Romans directly ruled the regions of Judea and Samaria. Archelaus, one of the sons of Herod assigned to Judea and Samaria by the Romans, would prove inept and excessively cruel, and would be deposed by the Romans in AD 6. From then on, the Romans would rule this key area from their base in Caesarea Maritima on the Mediterranean coast, a harbor city constructed by Herod the Great from 22 to 10 BC. Thus, the stage was set for the complicated intersection of the Jewish religious authorities and the Roman procurator in deciding the fate of Jesus.

While the Gospels portray the public ministry of Jesus as confined to Galilee and to Jerusalem and its surrounding region, the Acts of the Apostles, as we will see, identifies Caesarea Maritima and various cities in the coastal region as entwined with the early mission of the Jerusalem church and the climax of Paul's own destiny as apostle to the Gentiles.[7]

CLIMATE AND RAINFALL

These diverse regions of the Holy Land experienced some variety of climate, including the vital element of rainfall. In general, the entire region has two basic seasons, the "dry" season that stretches from early spring (March) to the fall (October), and the "rainy," or winter, season from late October and early November to late March or early April. But rainfall is by no means distributed evenly over the various regions of the land. Generally, there is more rainfall in the elevated northern regions and in the hill country of the central highlands. In the Galilee region, as the Gospels and Jesus's choice of imagery reflect, there is lush, almost semitropical vegetation and an abundance of flowers and springs. Abundant rainfall, fertile alluvial soil in the plains, and basalt soil around the sea ensure lush foliage and productive agriculture.

The coastal areas benefit from the moisture coming from the Mediterranean. But as the elevation of the land descends from the Judean highlands toward the Rift Valley to the east and into the Negev to the south, there is a sharp decline in average rainfall and consequently in the ability of the land to support agriculture. The way of life of the desert-dwelling people, including the nomads, or Bedouin, of modern times, is a constant search for water and enough food to sustain them through the driest periods of the year. God's biblical promise of a "land of milk and honey" assumes arable land and adequate rainfall to enable the raising of sheep, goats, and cattle ("milk") and land fertile with enough moisture to grow blossoming orchards and crops ("honey"). From the Bible's point of view, the desert was a temporary sojourn for Israel, not its ultimate goal.

THE RATIONALE AND PLAN OF THIS STUDY

Highlighting this "spiritual landscape" of the Gospels and the Acts of the Apostles, a landscape forged both by geography and history as well as theology, is the goal of this book. The general outline of this inquiry is fairly straightforward. After describing the lay of the land of the overall biblical arena, that is, the lands in which the biblical drama took place, we will turn to each of the Gospels and note the role geography and its symbolic dimensions plays in adding layers of meaning to the gospel message. Since Mark's Gospel serves as the primary source for the Gospels of Matthew and Luke, we will linger more over Mark's spiritual landscape, and then highlight the distinctive features to be found in Matthew and Luke. In the case of Luke's Gospel, the geographical landscape of the second volume of his work, the Acts of the Apostles, projects the Christian mission out into the wider Mediterranean world. This wider geographical perspective is strongly alluded to in the other three Gospels, but because their accounts are limited to the time and place of Jesus's mission, it is not presented in the bold and explicit terms of Luke's narrative. We will consider the Acts of the Apostles along with the Gospel of Luke, moving Acts out of its canonical order, to illustrate the continuity between these two key New Testament texts.

John's Gospel, here as in virtually every other dimension of its portrayal of Jesus, has a geographical landscape notably different from the Synoptics, even though the Johannine Jesus, too, is firmly rooted in the biblical land. John also moves the journey of Jesus's life and destiny to a cosmic or spatial sphere, portraying the origin of the Word in the life of God, its descent into the realm of the "flesh," and the return of the triumphant Christ to God projected at the end of the Gospel.

We might call what we are attempting to do "mapping" the Gospels. Good maps help us get from one place to another and can give us a sense of what our journey might entail as it navigates various towns and cities, or crosses rivers and mountain passes. "Mapping" the Gospels means moving through their narratives, being attentive to the significance of the terrain and the places the evangelists include in the journey of Jesus. The approach we are taking does not claim to be a full commentary on these biblical texts but, hopefully, points to another important dimension of their overall message.

I have had the privilege of teaching in and traveling throughout the biblical lands over many years, including the joy of introducing hundreds of other Christians to an experience of the Holy Land, an arena that includes not only present-day Israel, Palestine, Jordan, Syria, and Lebanon, but also Greece, Turkey, and Egypt—and in the cases of Peter and Paul, places like Malta and Rome. Found in these biblical lands are an incredible history, beautiful and evocative landscapes, and great, hospitable people. Most of these lands, sadly, are laced with conflict, violence, and dire poverty, but they are proud of their heritage and well aware of their privilege to welcome peoples from around the world who come as pilgrims to visit the abundance of sacred places that exist in their homelands. To them, the peoples of the biblical lands and to the many friends I have found there over the years, this book is dedicated.

CHAPTER ONE

The Landscape of the Gospel of Mark

The Gospel of Mark was probably the first Gospel to be written. The narrative pattern provided by Mark's Gospel, including its overall landscape, sets the pattern for the Gospels of Matthew and Luke, who, in the view of most biblical scholars, used Mark as their primary source.

We cannot be sure of the exact date when Mark's Gospel was composed or where it first appeared. However, the traditional view that Mark's Gospel originated in Rome around the year AD 70, in the wake of the persecution of the Christian community there by the Emperor Nero, has a strong probability. Such a context, a community battered by a brutal persecution, would help explain some of the tone of Mark's Gospel, with its portrayal of Jesus confronting the raw power of evil in his healings and exorcisms and with the Gospel's focus on the passion of Jesus. Striking, too, is the way Mark portrays Jesus's disciples as chronically dull and uncomprehending in the face of Jesus's teaching, particularly his teaching about "giving his life in order to find it." Eventually, overcome by fear, they abandon Jesus at the moment of his arrest and trial. Only the initiative of the risen Christ renews their discipleship and restores them to their original mission of proclaiming the gospel. Their plight, too, evokes the circumstances of a community battered by persecution and, in some cases, experiencing failure and betrayal.

Although Mark's narrative may have been composed some forty years after the death and resurrection of Jesus and in the imperial capital, the evangelist places the story of Jesus within the setting of early first-century Palestine. We cannot be sure that the composer of the Gospel in fact had set foot in the Holy Land, but the materials from which he composed his Gospel certainly retained geographical, cultural, and political memories from the time and place of Jesus's life. In drawing up the "landscape" of his Gospel, Mark was also conscious of the backdrop provided by the Old Testament. Jesus is presented by Mark—as he is by all four Gospels—as the fulfillment of the hopes of Israel and its Scriptures. Thus some aspects of the Gospel's landscape derive additional meaning because of their resonance with the events and motifs of the Old Testament.

Our goal here is to track certain features of the landscape in which Mark situates the story of Jesus that give deeper meaning to the Gospel narrative. We can take our cue from the major areas or geographical arenas that appear successively in Mark's account: (1) the Judean wilderness; (2) Galilee; (3) the journey from Galilee to Jerusalem; (4) Jerusalem and its temple; and (5) the return to Galilee.

THE WILDERNESS BEGINNING

The opening scene of Mark's Gospel (1:1–13) takes place in the "desert," which the evangelist locates as the "Judean countryside" at the Jordan River.[1] Using a combined Old Testament quotation, Mark introduces John the Baptist, as "the voice of one crying out in the desert," calling Israel to prepare the "way of the Lord" and "proclaiming a baptism of repentance for the forgiveness of sins." John's role is to introduce Jesus, the messianic "stronger one" who will baptize not simply with water but with the Spirit. Mark's description of John, clothed in camel's hair and eating locusts and wild honey, evokes the memory of Elijah, the great prophet of ancient Israel who had been taken up into heaven and was expected to return at the end of time. Elijah, too, had gone to the desert wilderness, fleeing from the wrath of Ahab and Jezebel in the north of Israel, and had encountered God at Mount Horeb in the Sinai (1 Kgs 19). This beginning of Mark's narrative underscores that the advent of Jesus marks a decisive turn in human history.

In its own right, the desert is a dramatic landscape, spare and ascetical, devoid of the comforts of human habitation and challenging those who enter it. The biblical memories Mark's Gospel evokes add additional layers of meaning. Between God's miraculous liberation of Israel from the yoke of Pharaoh's slavery in Egypt and the entrance into the promised land is the desert sojourn. Part of this sojourn was simply geographic necessity — to move from Egypt to Canaan required crossing the Sinai desert bridge between the two regions. But what was intended as a movement from slavery to freedom through the desert is, in the Bible's view, thwarted by Israel's hesitation and doubt. The spies who reconnoiter the land God had promised to Israel return in panic at the fearsome foes who await them in this land. As a result, Israel is condemned to wander for forty years in the desert, a time both of testing and failure — the idolatry of the golden calf — but also of a unique intimacy with God, with Moses's encounter with the Lord on Sinai and the forging of a covenant with Israel.[2] Only after this long desert sojourn and the trek up the eastern side of the Rift Valley would Israel be ready to descend into the valley and cross the Jordan River into their land of promise.

Mark also sets up a contrast that will be strongly developed in the body of his narrative, namely the contrast between Galilee and Jerusalem. John's dramatic preaching draws people from "the whole Judean countryside and all the inhabitants of Jerusalem" who come to confess their sins (1:5). Both Matthew and Luke openly question the sincerity of these Judeans. Mark, without commenting on the Judeans' intentions, introduces Jesus, who comes "from Nazareth of Galilee" (1:9) to be baptized in the Jordan. Jesus's baptism in the Jordan is, in fact, a theophany, as he emerges from the waters that in the Bible mark the boundary of the promised land, the heavens are split open and the voice of God declares, "You are my beloved Son; with you I am well pleased" (1:10–11). Identified as God's unique Son, the Spirit-filled Jesus is literally "driven" or "cast" farther out into the desert. Here again Mark draws on Old Testament symbolism. In the starkness of the desert, Jesus encounters raw evil and "for forty days" is "tested" (a better translation of the Greek verb *peirasomenos* than "tempted") by Satan. This wordless encounter is, in fact, an overture to the Gospel as a whole. Jesus will confront the power of evil that wounds human bodies and spirits, bringing isolation and death. But through the power of the Spirit of God, Jesus will liberate God's sons and daughters from the grip of evil — the very purpose of his mission.

That victory is hinted at in Mark's description of the outcome of Jesus's testing: "He was among the wild beasts, and the angels ministered to him" (1:13). Unlike Israel, who repeatedly failed its desert tests, Jesus the Galilean is faithful and triumphant. Being at ease with the wild beasts and the presence of ministering angels recalls the paradise visions of the Old Testament such as Isaiah 11 and 66, which portray the end-time as the "peaceable kingdom" where all creation is reconciled. Where Israel faltered in its desert test, Jesus would not. His triumph over the power of Satan anticipates the liberating force of his entire mission, which he would begin in Galilee.

GALILEE AND THE MISSION OF JESUS

Galilee is the main arena for Jesus's ministry in the Gospel of Mark (1:14 — 8:21). After the mythic opening scenes of the narrative, involving voices from heaven and a confrontation with Satan in the desert, Jesus returns to his home region, where the evangelist states the keynote of Jesus's mission: "After John had been arrested, Jesus came to Galilee proclaiming the gospel of God: 'This is the time of fulfillment. The kingdom of God is at hand. Repent, and believe in the gospel'" (Mark 1:14-15).

As noted earlier, the geographical region of Galilee, whose name in Hebrew simply means the "district," includes the northern mountainous area of Upper Galilee, and the lower elevation of Lower Galilee, dominated by the Sea of Galilee on its eastern side and the fertile Jezreel Valley running west to the Carmel range.

Mark's Portrayal of Jesus's Galilean Mission

Key features of Jesus's Galilean mission as portrayed in Mark fit the unique landscape and history of this region.[3] Although Mark identifies Nazareth in western Galilee as Jesus's hometown (referred to in 6:1 as Jesus's *patrida*, or place of origin), his base of operations is clearly Capernaum, a fishing village on the northwest corner of the Sea of Galilee. It is here, according to Mark, that Jesus established his "home" (*oikos*, see 2:1), although the narrative does not make clear if Jesus had his own dwelling or, what is more likely, took shelter with one of his disciples who lived there.

Healings in Synagogues and Villages

Mark situates the first public act of Jesus's ministry in the synagogue of Capernaum on a Sabbath (1:21-28), where he liberates a man convulsed with "an unclean spirit," the first of many exorcisms characteristic of Jesus's mission in Mark's Gospel. The same powerful Spirit that drove Jesus into the desert to confront the power of Satan will drive his liberating and healing ministry throughout the region of Galilee and beyond, to additional villages and areas named in Mark such as Bethsaida, Dalmanutha, and Genneseret. Mark follows this opening scene with a day-long series of healings, including Simon's mother-in-law and then, later that evening when the Sabbath was concluded, a stream of suffering people brought to Jesus for healing, with the "whole town...gathered at the door" where Jesus performed his powerful acts (1:32–34). Early the next morning after praying in a "deserted place," Jesus tells his disciples he must go to the "nearby villages" to proclaim the good news of God's reign, which Mark summarizes: "So he went into their synagogues, preaching and driving out demons throughout the whole of Galilee" (1:39). The emotional healing of a leper serves as a climactic point in this intense healing activity, the report of which forced Jesus to seek "deserted places," but "people kept coming to him from everywhere" (1:45).

THE SEA

Another important arena for Jesus's Galilean ministry is the Sea of Galilee, referred to in most literature of the era as the "lake" but in the Gospels usually as the "sea" (in Greek, *thallase*), perhaps evoking the profound and mysterious dimensions of the greater "sea," such as the Mediterranean, played in ancient mythology.[4] Many of the events that in Mark's account take place on the "Sea of Galilee" have that mysterious and frightening quality.

The very first act of Jesus (1:16–20) is to call as his disciples Simon and Andrew, James and John, all of whom are fishermen plying their trade, casting and mending their nets by the Sea. At Jesus's command to "follow him" and become "fishers of men," without a word they leave behind their nets and, in the case of the Sons of Zebedee, their father. The call of Levi the tax collector from Capernaum also takes place "along the sea" (2:13). In what is called by some commentators Mark's "great summary" of Jesus's ministry, the evangelist describes Jesus withdrawing "toward the sea" after a severe confrontation with his Pharisee opponents (3:7–12). Mark portrays great crowds drawn to Jesus from the entire span of the Holy Land: "from Jerusalem, from Idumea [i.e., southwestern Jordan], from beyond the Jordan [i.e., the eastern side of the Jordan Valley], and from the neighborhood of Tyre and Sidon [near the Mediterranean coast north of Israel]." So great is the crowd that Jesus instructs his disciples "to have a boat ready for him because of the crowd, so that they would not crush him." Similarly at the beginning of the parable discourse in Mark, Jesus will be teaching by the sea again when the press of the crowd eager to hear him leads Jesus to get into a boat and teach the crowds fanned out in front of him, no doubt in the natural coves that mark the shoreline in the northwest corner of the sea (4:1).

Some of the most remarkable events in Mark's portrayal of Jesus's Galilean ministry take place on or near the sea. Both accounts of the feeding of the multitudes are framed with Jesus and his disciples crossing the sea. In the first, Jesus and his disciples go off by boat to a deserted place in order to rest (6:30–32); the precise location is not indicated. Upon disembarking, Jesus sees the vast crowds that have followed him and, "moved with pity," determines to teach them and later to feed them, over the protests of his disciples, who want to send them away (6:34–44). After the crowds have been fed to satisfaction — with twelve baskets of fragments left over — Jesus sends his disciples by boat "to the other side toward Bethsaida" while he dismisses the crowd and then goes off to "the mountain to pray." Bethsaida is another fishing village similar to Capernaum on the northern shore of the sea, where Jesus would later heal a blind man (8:22–26).[5]

Mark seems to situate the second feeding story somewhere in the Decapolis region on the eastern side of the Sea, thus in Gentile territory.[6] After Jesus's foray into the region of Tyre and Sidon (see below), Mark notes that he returns to the Sea of Galilee "into the district of the Decapolis" (7:31), where he heals a man who is both deaf and mute (7:31–37), and with another great crowd gathered, is driven by compassion to feed them (8:1–9). In this instance, "seven" baskets of fragments remain. When the feeding is complete, Mark notes that Jesus and his disciples again get into a boat "and [come] to the region of Dalmanutha," that is, on the western or Jewish side of the lake (8:10). The location of this second feeding story in Gentile territory and the symbolic number seven, usually implying infinity, along with the twelve baskets remaining from the first feeding story, which was in Jewish territory, clearly indicate that Mark sees Jesus's miraculous feeding of the multitudes as an anticipation of the postresurrection Gentile mission, incorporating both Jew and Gentile. The accounts themselves are filled with symbolism, the "deserted place" evoking memory of God's feeding the people with manna in the desert trek of Israel while the gestures of Jesus, who "gave thanks, broke...and distribute[d]" the loaves, anticipate the Lord's Supper or Eucharist to come.

Both of Mark's sea stories draw on the physical reality of the Sea of Galilee as vulnerable to rapidly developing storms, situated as it is in a basin surrounded by mountains. But equally important, the tone of the stories draw on the symbolic meaning attached to the sea in the Bible. The sea is viewed as the abode of the demonic, a mysterious realm of sudden chaos and threat over which God alone has power (see, e.g., Ps 107:23–32; 148:7; Job 9:8).

The first sea story is the stilling of the storm in Mark 4:35–41. While a "violent squall" threatens to sink the boat, Jesus sleeps in the stern. The terrified disciples rouse Jesus and he "rebuke[s] the wind" and calms the sea, in effect overpowering the threat of the sea in a manner similar to his driving out demons from the people they torture. The story concludes with Jesus challenging the disciples on their lack of faith, and with the disciples themselves wondering, "Who then is this whom even wind and sea obey"? —a power that the Bible attributes to God alone (see, e.g., Exod 14:21; Ps 135:7; Job 38:22–30).

In the second dramatic sea event (6:45–52), Jesus comes to the disciples walking on the water while they are also in distress on the sea, "tossed about while rowing, for the wind was against them." Here, too, the physical reality of a sea storm becomes the setting for a profound symbolic and theological assertion. Jesus identified himself with the divine name, *Ego Eimi*—"I am"— cited in Isaiah (see, e.g., Isa 42:8; 43:11; 45:5) and treads upon the crests of the sea in a manner attributed to Yahweh (see Job 9:8). His words of assurance—"Take courage…do not be afraid"—are met with incomprehension on the part of the disciples, a lack of faith and understanding that the evangelist links to their failure to understand the multiplication of the loaves: "They had not understood the incident of the loaves. On the contrary, their hearts were hardened" (6:52).

BEYOND GALILEE…HINTS OF THE GENTILE MISSION

Mark uses the geographical and ethnic landscape of Galilee to anticipate that Jesus's mission would eventually extend beyond the boundaries of Israel. In chapter 5, Mark presents the longest exorcism story in his entire Gospel, the healing of the Gerasene demoniac. Mark's account underscores the Gentile setting for this story. Jesus and his disciples go "to the other side" of the lake, the territory of the Gerasenes. The precise location is uncertain; an alternate reading identifies the place as "Gadara," one of the cities of the Decapolis, but without question it is non-Jewish territory. The tormented man overpowered by demons lives among the tombs and is possessed by demonic powers who identify themselves as *legio*, a Latin word signifying "many," but also a loan word that evokes the presence of Roman troops beyond the Golan in this same eastern region. We learn later that Jesus drives the demons out of the man and into a herd of pigs, another sure sign of Gentile territory, who, in turn, plunge into the sea, a worthy abode of the demonic. When the Gerasene, now fully healed and restored to human life, begs to follow Jesus back across the sea, Jesus instead instructs the man, "Go home to your family and announce to them all that the Lord in his pity has done for you." Then, Mark notes, "The man went off and begin to proclaim in the Decapolis what Jesus had done for him; and all were amazed" (5:19-20)—clearly a sign of the Gentile mission yet to come!

The unusual story of Jesus's encounter with the Syrophoenician woman (7:24-30) is another example that anticipates the wider Gentile mission. Mark notes that Jesus "went off *to* [the Greek preposition *eis*] the district of Tyre," where he stays in a house to escape notice. But he is discovered by a woman who is "Greek, a Syrophoenician by birth," who requests that Jesus heal her daughter who was possessed by a demon. Jesus seems to rebuff her, emphasizing that his mission was first of all to the "children" of Israel and that it was not right to take the bread of the children and "throw it to the dogs." The woman refuses to be put off by this blunt rejection: "Lord, even the dogs under the table eat the children's scraps." Her reply changes Jesus's response and he tells her, "For saying this, you may go. The demon has gone out of your daughter." This story will be even more pointed in the Gospel of Matthew, where the question of navigating the Gentile mission is even more acute than in Mark's Gospel.[7] However, even here, the function of this story in widening the horizon of Jesus's messianic mission is clear.

After this encounter, Mark continues to place Jesus in Gentile territory: "Again he left the district of Tyre and went by way of Sidon to the Sea of Galilee, into the district of the Decapolis" (Mark 7:31). Commentators have pointed out that this itinerary is somewhat improbable. As a map of the region shows, it would be impractical but not impossible to travel from Tyre to Sidon and then to the Decapolis by way of the Sea of Galilee. Sidon is to the north of Tyre and the Decapolis is on the eastern shore of the Sea of Galilee. Whether or not the evangelist was familiar with the details of the region can be debated, but his intention in moving Jesus into Gentile territory is clear.

CONFLICT AND OPPOSITION IN GALILEE

There is no doubt that Mark situates the full scope of Jesus's dynamic mission of teaching and healing in Galilee, but this should not lead the reader of Mark to view Galilee in romantic terms as the ideal region where the mission of Jesus flourishes. Mark also portrays Galilee as a place where deadly opposition to Jesus occurs. After the first full day of healing in Capernaum (1:21–45), Jesus returns to his "home" to be confronted by his opponents in a series of conflict stories (2:1 – 3:6). In the final incident in the series, the Sabbath healing of the man with a withered arm in the synagogue (presumably the synagogue of Capernaum), his opponents "immediately took counsel...against him to put him to death" (3:6). Thus, Mark anticipates Jesus's death early in the Gospel narrative, a result of threats against Jesus that reoccur during his Galilean mission, including the accusations of "scribes who had come from Jerusalem" that Jesus is under the control of Beelzebul, the prince of demons (see 3:22).

CONCLUSION

Mark uses the landscape of Galilee to portray for the reader the full scope of Jesus's proclamation of the kingdom of God. Here in the villages and towns, in synagogues and in homes, the Spirit-filled Jesus casts out demons and restores human bodies and spirits to life. Here, too, he begins to form the fragile community of disciples who will ultimately be entrusted with his mission to the world. On the sea, the dominant feature of lower Galilee, Jesus's transcendent identity and saving power is revealed in quelling the storm and walking on the water. In the stories of feeding the multitudes on the shores of the sea, Jesus again reveals the nature of his mission, evoking memories of Yahweh's liberation of his people Israel in the desert, anticipating the Lord's Supper, and revealing God's inclusive embrace of Jew and Gentile that will drive the future Christian mission. But here, too, the ultimate cost of Jesus's mission is anticipated in the deadly opposition to him that begins to build at the very beginning of his work in Galilee. The shadow of the cross already falls across the landscape of Jesus's Galilean mission.

TURNING POINT – THE JOURNEY TO JERUSALEM

A major turning point in Mark's Gospel narrative takes place toward the end of chapter 8, and once again the landscape plays a significant role. Commentators have noted some defining literary features of this section of Mark's Gospel that stretches from 8:21 to 10:52. First of all, the entire section is presented as a journey of Jesus and his disciples, beginning in the far northern region of Caesarea Philippi, moving eventually down the Jordan River valley, then through Jericho and on up the traditional ascent to Jerusalem. The Greek word *hodos*, meaning "journey" or the "way," occurs throughout this section. This had already been sounded as a motif in the opening lines of Mark's Gospel in the citation from Isaiah, announcing the advent of John the Baptist and his mission of "prepar[ing] the way [*hodos*] of the Lord" (Mark 1:2-3). The metaphor of a "journey" has its roots in the great biblical journey of Israel from slavery in Egypt to the promised land. For the Gospel, the "journey" becomes a metaphor for the unfolding experience of Christian life itself.

Some commentators consider it significant that Mark begins the journey in "the villages of Caesarea Philippi" (8:27). This area forms the northern border of the Holy Land in Upper Galilee, but it was also the site of several pagan shrines, including a shrine to the Greek god Pan at the very place where the headwaters of the Jordan emerge from the mountainside. It is here that Jesus asks his disciples the fundamental question: "Who do you say that I am?" (8:29). Was Mark or the traditional source of his account aware that

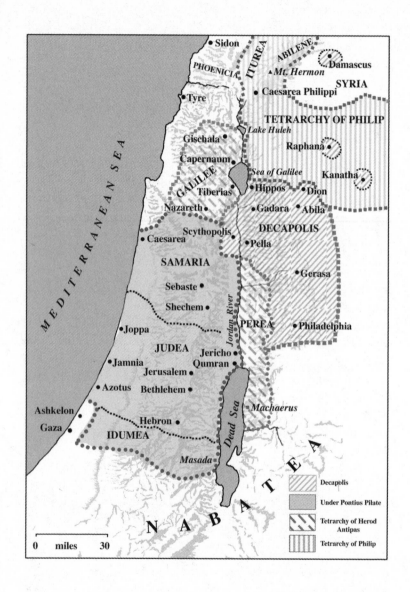

this region was a pagan cult site and Jesus's question is posed in the light of that setting? Or is the evangelist and his source simply wanting to place Jesus in the upper reaches of Galilee as the beginning spot for the long journey to Jerusalem? We cannot be sure.

The dramatic scene at Caesarea Philippi is followed shortly by another epic incident ("after six days," Mark 9:2), the transfiguration of Jesus (9:2–8), which takes place on a "high mountain" whose precise location is not identified. Clearly the mountain setting for this revelation of Jesus's transcendent identity has a strong symbolic dimension, with the presence with Jesus of Moses the great lawgiver and Elijah the prophet of the end-time, and, as at Mount Sinai, there is a theophany, with a voice speaking from the cloud surrounding the mountain: "This is my beloved Son. Listen to him." This affirmation of Jesus's unique identity recalls the opening scene of the Gospel and prepares the reader for the orientation to the passion of Jesus and the instructions on discipleship that will take place during this fateful journey to Jerusalem.

As the Gospel narrative unfolds, Mark plots the journey in general terms: Jesus and his disciples "begin a journey through Galilee" (9:30), pass again through Capernaum (9:33), then move south toward Judea taking the valley route "across the Jordan" (10:1), pass through Jericho (10:46), and continue on to Jerusalem. Two stories of the healing of blindness frame the entire journey narrative. In the healing of the blind man in the village of Bethsaida (8:22–26), the man's condition seems deep seated and Jesus must work a second time to fully restore his sight. The other story, occurring at the very end of the section as Jesus passes through Jericho and begins the ascent up to Jerusalem (10:46–52), is that of the healing of Bartimaeus. Here the blind man takes the initiative to approach Jesus, leaving aside his garments and declaring, "Master, I want to see." Once his eyes are opened, Mark's account notes that Bartimaeus "followed [Jesus] on the way." This healing story is, in fact, a discipleship story. Both healings form an apt framework for a section of the Gospel where the "blindness" of the disciples regarding Jesus's teaching and example will become painfully clear.

For Mark the "journey" from Galilee to Jerusalem is also a journey to the cross. A defining feature of this section of the narrative is the series of three dramatic passion predictions (8:31; 9:30–31; 10:32–34), each followed by an example of the failure of the disciples to comprehend Jesus's teaching. Jesus, in turn, further instructs his disciples on the imperative of giving one's life in service in order to truly find it—a lesson captured in some of the most demanding discipleship instructions in all of the Gospel.

The "landscape" of this section changes the dynamic of Mark's narrative. The profusion of Jesus's exorcisms and healings in Galilee give way to a focus on Jesus's teaching his disciples. The series of travels Jesus undertakes during his ministry to the Galilean village and the multiple crossings of the Sea of Galilee turn now to a single purposeful journey to Jerusalem where Jesus will give his life: "For the Son of Man did not come to be served but to serve and to give his life as a ransom for many" (10:45). Even though they do not yet fully comprehend Jesus and his mission, the disciples must take up this journey with him to Jerusalem and to the cross before they will be ready to proclaim the gospel.

JERUSALEM

The arrival of Jesus and his disciples in the vicinity of Jerusalem marks the beginning of the final major section of the Gospel, stretching from the actions in the temple (chs. 11 – 12), then to Jesus's discourse about the future of the community on the Mount of Olives (ch. 13), and finally to the passion narrative itself (chs. 14 – 15). The climax of Jesus's mission is about to take place in the city that, since the time of King David in the tenth century BC, was viewed by the Jews as the center of Jewish life and identity.[8]

BETHANY

Mark's narrative places Jesus's activity in several key areas. The village of Bethany on the eastern slopes of the Mount of Olives near the city of Jerusalem is portrayed as the place where Jesus stays while he in Jerusalem. This is, in fact, true of all four Gospels. John will portray Jesus as residing in the home of his friends, Lazarus and his sisters Martha and Mary (John 11:1). Mark is less precise about where Jesus stays in Bethany, although the incident of the anointing of Jesus by an anonymous woman takes place while Jesus is dining "in the house of Simon the leper" (Mark 14:3). In any case, Bethany is the place of refuge for Jesus outside of Jerusalem proper and he returns there to spend the night after

his dramatic entrance into the city and its temple (11:11–12), as well as after his prophetic action in cleansing the temple (11:19). When Jesus apparently attempts to return to Bethany after celebrating the Passover with his disciples ("After singing a hymn, they went out to the Mount of Olives," 14:26), he is arrested while praying in the Garden of Gethsemane, traditionally located in the Kidron Valley, which separates the eastern side of the temple area from the Mount of Olives (see John 18:1).

Once again, landscape helps amplify the meaning of Mark's narrative. While Bethany is a place of refuge, Jerusalem and its temple are portrayed as a zone of conflict and opposition. The anointing of Jesus in Bethany on the very eve of his passion is indicative of the contrast. While the religious leaders (i.e., "the chief priests and the scribes") in Jerusalem plot to arrest Jesus (14:1–2) and one of his own disciples decides to betray him to the "chief priests" (14:10–11), an unnamed woman of Bethany anoints Jesus's head with precious ointment, an action that Jesus himself interprets as something "beautiful" and as a preparation for his burial (14:3–9). Her act of reverence for Jesus receives a recognition singular in all the New Testament: "Amen, I say to you, wherever the gospel is proclaimed to the whole world, what she has done will be told in memory of her" (14:9).

THE TEMPLE

A major setting in this finale of the Gospel is obviously the temple. This was the magnificent temple that had been rebuilt by Herod the Great, beginning in 19 BC; at its completion, shortly before its tragic destruction during the Jewish revolt against Rome in AD 70, it was the second largest human structure in the world, with only the temple complex of Karnak in Egypt exceeding it.[9] Its magnificence is acknowledged by Jesus's disciples as they view the temple looming in front of them from the crest of the Mount of Olives: "Look, teacher, what stones and what buildings!"

(Mark 13:1). Yet Mark's Gospel portrays the temple in decidedly negative tones. Mark frames Jesus's prophetic action cleansing the temple (11:15–19) with the story of the fig tree that is condemned by Jesus for not producing fruit (11:12–14, 20–25), suggesting that this Herodian version of the temple would ultimately be destroyed and replaced by a worthy place of worship. This, in fact, is explicitly stated by Jesus in his final discourse on the Mount of Olives: "Do you see these great buildings? There will not be one stone left upon another that will not be thrown down" (13:2). This prediction is turned into an accusation against Jesus during his trial before the Sanhedrin: "We heard him say, 'I will destroy this temple made with hands and within three days I will build another not made with hands'" (14:58).

The scenes taking place in the temple throughout chapters 11 and 12 of Mark's narrative continue this negative tone. The various opponents of Jesus—the "chief priests, the scribes, and the elders" (11:27), along with the "Pharisees and the Herodians" (12:13) and the "Sadducees" (12:18)—all in turn come forward to challenge Jesus while he is teaching in the temple precincts. Mark's vantage point, writing to a majority Gentile audience probably in Rome and most likely after the destruction of the temple, drains the Jerusalem temple of its religious significance. It is now viewed as a locus of opposition to Jesus and a place whose religious integrity has been thoroughly compromised by the religious leaders who have made it a "den of thieves" (Mark 11:17). It is not the temple itself that Mark condemns—he is surely aware from the Scriptures of the innate holiness of the temple as the place where God uniquely dwelt. His negative tone is sparked by the religious leaders' rejection of Jesus and what the evangelist interprets as their lack of sincerity. The final scene in the temple portrayed by Mark (12:38–44) contrasts the wholehearted devotion of the widow who is praised by Jesus because she gives "all she had" to the temple treasury, while the "scribes" are condemned for seeking honor but "devour the houses of widows."

THE MOUNT OF OLIVES

Mark situates the final discourse of Jesus on the Mount of Olives (13:3). Earlier it was from the Mount of Olives that Jesus had begun his dramatic entry into the Holy City, with the crowds acclaiming Jesus:

> Hosanna!
>> Blessed is he who comes in the name of the Lord!
>> Blessed is the kingdom of our father David that is
>> to come!
> Hosanna in the highest! (11:9–10)

Jewish tradition considered this mountain, which looms to the east of Jerusalem and separates the city from the arid land that begins to descend rapidly toward the Rift Valley, as the place of the final judgment. The tradition is apparently based on the text in the prophet Zechariah, who in his description of the end time notes, "On that day God's feet will stand on the Mount of Olives, which is opposite Jerusalem to the east" (Zech 14:4). This prophecy may be the reason that the Mount of Olives has been the location of a Jewish cemetery for almost three thousand years. In any case, it is here that Jesus speaks to his disciples about the destruction of the temple and the cataclysms that will engulf the community as it moves out into history. The purpose of Jesus's discourse is not to incite apocalyptic fever about an early end to the world but to dampen it—in the view of Mark's Gospel, despite the lure of false prophets who declare otherwise, the end cannot come before the gospel has been proclaimed "to all nations" (13:10). In the meantime, Jesus exhorts his followers to "stay awake," alert for the final triumph of the Son of Man's return.

THE DRAMA OF THE PASSION

Mark's passion account takes up the whole of chapters 14–15 and is the longest sequential narrative in his Gospel. Several scenes form the landscape of the passion narrative and help set its tone.

THE UPPER ROOM

After the anointing at Bethany and Mark's references to the plot of the religious leaders and the betrayal of Judas (14:1–11), the opening scene is that of Jesus's final Passover meal with his disciples. The location is a "large upper room furnished and ready," a "guest room" belonging to a man the disciples sent by Jesus are to encounter "in the city" (14:12–16). In Mark's account, Jesus uses the setting of the Passover meal to interpret his impending death as his body "broken" for them and the cup of wine as his "blood of the covenant, which will be shed for many" (14:22–24). Here, too, Jesus would poignantly predict the failure of his disciples when faced with the threat of death. Later tradition locates this "upper room" in the area of "New Sion" on the crest of the hill forming the western side of Jerusalem, a not improbable location but not one pinpointed in Mark's more generalized description.

GETHSEMANE

Following the meal, Jesus and his disciples set out for "the Mount of Olives" (14:26), presumably to return to Bethany. On the way Jesus pauses for prayer in a "place named Gethsemane" — the name derived from the Hebrew *Gat Shmanim*, meaning "oil press." This has been traditionally located in the Kidron Valley, which separates the temple mount from the Mount of Olives, a setting that fits Mark's account. What Mark seems to describe as an olive grove, John's account refers to as a "garden" (John 18:1). In any case it is here, halfway between Jerusalem and Bethany, that Jesus's encounter with the forces of death begins. Judas, his betrayer, leads a "crowd with swords and clubs who had come from the chief priests, the scribes, and the elders" (Mark 14:43) to seize Jesus and, at the same time, precipitate the flight of the disciples, including in Mark's account, a young man who flees naked, leaving his linen clothing behind (14:51–52).

THE HIGH PRIEST'S RESIDENCE

From this point on, the passion landscape moves first to the realm of the Jewish religious leaders and then to that of the Roman authorities. Jesus is first taken to the residence of the high priest, a dwelling that includes a "courtyard below" and an upper gathering place for the Sanhedrin, a council of the religious leaders. Mark's account does not provide a precise location for the high priest's residence, but presumably it was also on the upper slopes of the western ridge of Jerusalem where modern archaeology has located the remains of larger villas. Important for Mark's drama, however, is that this is the realm of the Jewish religious authorities who have been opposed to Jesus and will now condemn him. Compounding the anguish is that here, too, Peter, the lone disciple of Jesus remaining behind, publicly denies his discipleship when confronted by "one of the high priests's maids" (14:66). Mark stages the scene so that at the moment Jesus in the upper chamber confesses his identity as "the Messiah, the son of the Blessed One" (14:62), Peter in the courtyard below denies he even knows Jesus. After a nighttime interrogation, Mark describes the Sanhedrin meeting again at dawn to formally condemn Jesus and to hand him over to the Romans (15:1).

THE ROMAN PRAETORIUM

Jesus is now taken from the high priest's residence to what Mark identifies as the "praetorium" (15:16). This term originally referred to the tent of the "praetor," a high Roman magistrate, but later was applied to administrative or military center buildings. In Mark's description this is where Jesus would encounter Pontius Pilate, the Roman prefect who served from AD 26 to 36. Direct Roman rule over Judea and Samaria began after Herod the

Great's son Archaelaus was deposed in AD 6 because of his cruelty and ineptness. The seat of Roman power was located at Caesarea Maritima, the harbor city originally built by Herod the Great on the Mediterranean coast in 22–10 BC. Normally, the Roman prefects would come to Jerusalem only on special occasions such as the Feast of Passover, when great crowds would swell the city's population and require additional oversight on the part of the Roman occupiers. Formerly, historians had assumed that Pilate would reside at the Antonia fortress, the large tower-like structure that was built into the northwest corner of the temple enclosure. It is more likely, however, that Pilate would reside not in the barracks-like Antonia fortress but in the more commodious palace constructed earlier by Herod the Great and located near what is the present-day Jaffa Gate, on the crest of the western hill of Jerusalem.

The religious leaders vent their accusations against Jesus and incite the crowds to demand his crucifixion, the supreme Roman capital punishment, especially for crimes of sedition.[10] Although Mark is not as explicit as John's Gospel is, it appears that the "trial" before Pilate takes place in the open outside the praetorium itself. At first resistant, Pilate finally relents and condemns Jesus to death. But first there is another cruel episode inside the praetorium. Mark indicates that Roman soldiers "led him away inside the palace, that is, the praetorium, and assembled the whole cohort" (15:16). A Roman "cohort" (*speiran* in Greek) could be as many as six hundred soldiers, but it is likely that Mark simply wants to indicate a large gathering of troops who mock and torture Jesus for his supposed pretentions to kingship, an irony for the Christian reader of Mark who knows Jesus is truly a "king" but one very different from the assumptions of the Romans.

Mark, followed generally by the other Gospels, assigns responsibility for the death of Jesus mainly to the Jewish religious authorities, but also notes the fact of Roman involvement in the condemnation and execution of Jesus. Unlike the religious leaders, however, the Gospels portray Pilate as somewhat reluctant to condemn Jesus and he only does so under pressure from the leaders and the crowds. However, it should be emphasized that nothing in the passion narratives justifies an attitude of anti-Semitism or holding God's people of all time responsible for the death of Jesus.

GOLGOTHA

The finale of the passion narrative moves to "the place of Golgotha," which Mark translates, "Place of the Skull." This ominous name indicates that it was probably the regular execution site; such sites were usually located outside the city walls but also in full public view. Roman law and practice saw crucifixion not only as punishment for the perpetrator but also as a deterrent for others. Mark's sober description of the final moments of Jesus's life accurately accords with what we know of the ritual of crucifixion, with the public march of the condemned to the place of execution, carrying at least the cross beam, with a placard indicating the crime for which they were condemned, the victims fastened to the cross often with nails but sometimes tied to it and subject to the ridicule of passing observers. The usually long final agony of the crucified and the degradation of being naked and in view of the passersby earned this form of capital punishment its description in antiquity as the "worst" form of execution (*mors turpissima crucis*).

On this landscape of death, Mark portrays the final breath of Jesus, a life totally poured out in act of loving service: "Jesus gave a loud cry and breathed his last" (15:37). A series of dramatic signs break out: the veil of the temple is torn in two; the centurion executioner acclaims Jesus as the Son of God; and the faithful women who had followed Jesus from Galilee and would become the witnesses to the empty tomb look on from a distance. While Mark portrays Jesus as fully experiencing the power of death, the life-giving Spirit that had animated Jesus in Galilee and brought him to Jerusalem would ultimately triumph over death.

FINALE: THE EMPTY TOMB AND THE RETURN TO GALILEE

The last scene in Mark's Gospel landscape is a rock-hewn tomb. As the eve of the Sabbath approaches, Joseph of Arimathea, whom Mark describes as "a distinguished member of the council, who was himself awaiting the kingdom of God" (15:43), asks Pilate for the crucified body of Jesus in order to place him in "a tomb that had been hewn out of the rock" (15:46). While Mark does not detail the location of the tomb, John's Gospel will situate it in a "garden" "in the place where he had been crucified" (John 19:41). To that tomb the women come on the Sunday morning following the Sabbath to anoint his broken body with spices. But what they discover is an empty tomb and a heavenly messenger who, in Mark's account, proclaims the resurrection of Jesus: "You seek Jesus of Nazareth, the crucified. He has been raised; he is not here" (16:6). Added to this astounding gospel news that by the power of God Jesus has triumphed over death, is a final promise: "But go and tell his disciples and Peter, 'He is going before you to Galilee; there you will see him, as he told you'" (16:7). That promise of reconciliation had been given to the disciples by Jesus himself at the Last Supper: "But after I have been raised up, I shall go before you to Galilee" (14:28). The women leave the empty tomb and with "trembling and bewilderment" carry this message of new life to the very disciples who had abandoned Jesus.

In Galilee they had been first called by Jesus and empowered by him to be "fishers of people." Emboldened by Jesus they would, in fact, proclaim the gospel and drive out demons, just as Jesus did (6:12–13, 30). But they would also lack understanding and balk at Jesus's message of service, of the necessity of giving one's life away in order to find it. And so they had to make the journey from Galilee to Jerusalem, experiencing their own weakness and need for conversion as the power of death swept over them. But now, through the forgiving love of the crucified and risen Jesus, they were called to return to Galilee to encounter him again and there to resume the mission of proclaiming the kingdom of God that he had entrusted to them.

The landscape of Mark's story helps give resonance and further meaning to his narrative: God's empowerment of his Son in the desert wilderness; Jesus's mission carried out in the synagogues and villages of Galilee; the haunting theophanies on the sea and on the mountaintop that signaled his transcendent power; the border crossings into Gentile territory that anticipated the Gentile mission to come; the long journey with his disciples from Caesarea to Jerusalem, a journey of challenge for his disciples; the move into Jerusalem, the heart of Judaism, with its moments of tenderness but also of encounters with opposition and ultimately the power of death itself; an empty tomb hewn out of rock that paradoxically becomes the place where the power of unending life is affirmed. The title of Mark's Gospel — "The beginning of the gospel of Jesus Christ [the Son of God]" (1:1) — would now come true.

CHAPTER TWO

The Landscape of the Gospel of Matthew

Matthew's Gospel bears the strong imprint of the landscape laid out by his prime source, the Gospel of Mark. Jesus's public ministry begins in Galilee and the climax of that ministry is in Jerusalem of Judea, while in between takes place the fateful journey of Jesus with his disciples from the far north of Galilee south to the Holy City. But, as we will trace, Matthew's landscape also has some unique features that amplify this Gospel's distinctive theology.

Matthew's portrayal of Jesus is influenced by two features that distinguish it from Mark. For one, Matthew and his community apparently had access to a second major source that was not incorporated into Mark's account. Named by modern biblical scholarship as the "Q" source, after the German word *Quelle*, which literally means "source," this apparently was a collection of sayings and parables of Jesus that Matthew and Luke had access to independently of each other. In Matthew's narrative most of this material is organized into a series of five discourses of Jesus.[1]

Matthew's distinctive perspective was also influenced by the historical circumstances of the community from which and for which this Gospel was first written. There is strong agreement among interpreters of Matthew that his Gospel was composed in the critical transition that engulfed early Christianity in the wake of the destruction of Jerusalem and its temple in AD 70. As we know already from Paul and other New Testament writings, the church had to navigate a profound transition from a birth in Judaism and its sacred traditions and customs to an increasingly Gentile membership and perspective. Matthew's Gospel, in particular, appears to directly address this challenging transition. Written for a primarily Jewish Christian audience but with an increasingly Gentile membership, Matthew's Gospel both affirms the Jewish roots of Jesus and his teaching and also wants to make room for the outreach of the gospel message to the "nations," that is, to the Gentile world. Matthew's Gospel may have been composed in Antioch, the third largest city of the Roman Empire. Located in present-day Turkey near the Syrian border, its first-century population included both Gentiles and Jews (Acts 11:19–30). As the Acts of the Apostles and Paul's own comments in his Letter to the Galatians (2:11–14) demonstrate, the transition from a predominantly Jewish to a predominantly Gentile Christian community was being played out in Antioch.

Several features of the geographical and historical landscape of Matthew's Gospel reflect this enormous pastoral change in the early church's life.

FROM EAST AND WEST: FEATURES OF MATTHEW'S INFANCY NARRATIVE

Different from Mark, Matthew's Gospel begins by tracing the origin of Jesus back to the time of his conception and infancy (Matthew 1–2). The opening genealogy establishes Jesus's Davidic pedigree (1:1–17) and prepares for the conception and birth of Jesus in Bethlehem, the ancestral city of David, the prototype of the royal Messiah or Anointed One whose identity Jesus will embody. This is an area never mentioned in the Gospel of

Mark. Unlike Luke's account, which seems to suppose that Mary and Joseph were already living in Nazareth and come to Bethlehem because of the requirements of a Roman census (see Luke 2:1–7), Matthew's traditions assume that Joseph and Mary originally were inhabitants of Bethlehem but go to Nazareth as refugees because of the threat posed by Archelaus, the son of Herod the Great who at the time ruled Judea (see below, Matt 2:21–23). Thus, already in the opening chapters of Matthew's account, the tension between Galilee and Jerusalem is anticipated.

FROM EAST TO WEST

Right from the start Matthew expands the landscape of Mark's account, to the east and to the west. "Magi from the east" come to Jerusalem seeking the "newborn king of the Jews" (Matt 2:1–2). The term *magoi* has Persian roots and usually referred to people with special knowledge or magic. Matthew describes them as astrologers who in searching the sky had discovered the portent of a special star. They come to Jerusalem to discover the precise location of the child and, despite Herod's treacherous attempts, pay homage to the "newborn king" in Bethlehem. This incident, unique to Matthew's Gospel, evokes two biblical traditions—one is the anticipated pilgrimage of the nations who will come in homage to Israel (see, e.g., Isa 60:4–9); Matthew will evoke this same tradition later in his account of the centurion who approaches Jesus asking healing for his servant (Matt 8:5–13). The fact that the Magi find indications of the Messiah by searching the stars also coincides with a conviction of the Wisdom tradition of Israel that one can find God's presence in the beauty and order of nature (a tradition cited by Paul in Rom 1:19–20).

Matthew's landscape extends not only to the east but to the west, namely to Egypt. The role of Joseph, who is alerted in a dream to take Jesus and Mary there (Matt 2:13–15), evokes another dimension of Egypt in the biblical saga. Egypt is remembered in

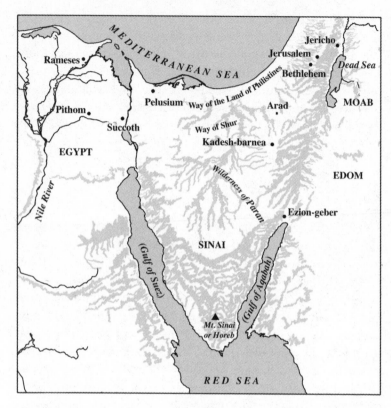

the Old Testament not only as the place of slavery leading up to the exodus, but earlier in the biblical story as a place of refuge for Jacob and his sons at a time of famine, rescued by another Joseph (see Gen 37 – 50). Thus Matthew's account recalls the entire span of the biblical arena that stretches from Persia or Mesopotamia in the northeast to Egypt in the southwest.[2]

GALILEE OF THE GENTILES

Matthew's narrative joins the gospel landscape of Mark with the appearance of John the Baptist and the baptism and testing scenes in the Judean desert (Matt 3:1 – 4:11). The sharp conflict between Jesus and the Jewish religious leaders breaks out again as the Baptist excoriates the "Pharisees and Sadducees" who come from Jerusalem to John for baptism in the Jordan River (Matt 3:7–12). Matthew, drawing on his "Q" source, expands the description of Jesus's temptations in the desert, with Satan taking Jesus to the "holy city" and the "parapet of the temple" as well as to "a very high mountain" (Matt 4:5-11), locations that will play a prominent role later in Matthew's account.

Although he will both add to and rearrange material found in Mark's description of Jesus's Galilean ministry, Matthew in general follows his prime source in portraying this region as the locus of Jesus's mission of teaching and healing. But there are changes in the landscape that stem from Matthew's own theological perspective.

To the Land of Israel First

The evangelist moves in two parallel tracks. First of all, Matthew affirms that Jesus's historical mission as the Jewish Messiah was confined to the land of Israel. Jesus has come not to "abolish the law or the prophets...but to fulfill" (Matt 5:17). Thus, Jesus instructs his disciples, "Do not go into pagan territory or enter a Samaritan town. Go rather to the lost sheep of the house of Israel" (10:5-6). This focus is repeated in the story of Jesus's encounter with the "Canaanite woman" (called a "Greek, a Syrophoenician" in Mark 7:26): "I was sent only to the lost sheep of the house of Israel" (Matt 15:24). Matthew follows through on this by several other subtle changes he makes in the landscape. The story of the healing of the Gadarene demoniac, which in Mark's version (5:1-20) is a clear anticipation of the Gentile mission, is muted by Matthew, who eliminates any mention of Jesus instructing the Gadarene to go off to the Decapolis proclaiming the gospel (see Matt 8:28-34; compare Mark 5:20). In the account of the Canaanite woman, Matthew also makes a subtle alternation. In Mark's version, Jesus goes into the district of Tyre and "enter[s] a house" where the woman learns of his presence and comes to him begging for healing for her daughter (Mark 7:24–30). Matthew's formulation implies that Jesus comes up to the region of Tyre—there is no mention of going into a house—and the woman "came" to see him when he is near the border (Matt 15:21–22). And Matthew's Jesus does not travel farther into the region of Tyre and Sidon as Mark describes (see Mark 7:31, omitted by Matthew). Likewise, Matthew does not follow Mark's account in accentuating that the two feedings of the crowds take place each in turn on the Jewish and Gentile sides of the Lake.

TO THE NATIONS

For Matthew's Gospel the full flowering of the mission to the Gentiles takes place at the very end of the Gospel, when the risen Christ signals that a new age of salvation has dawned (see 28:16–20). Yet, at the same time, Matthew makes clear early in his Gospel that the mission to the Gentiles is on the horizon. First of all, he underscores more explicitly than Mark the character of Galilee as a region whose history has cast it as an outlier within the framework of what was considered by some Jewish leaders as correct religious practice.[3] This is signaled in the very first verses describing Jesus's entry into Galilee: "He left Nazareth and went to live in Capernaum by the sea, in the region of Zebulun and Naphtali" (Matt 4:13). Matthew then cites the words of Isaiah (8:22 – 9:1):

> Land of Zebulun and land of Naphtali,
>> the way to the sea, beyond the Jordan,
>> Galilee of the Gentiles,
> the people who sit in darkness
>> have seen a great light,

on those dwelling in a land overshadowed
  by death
light has arisen. (Matt 4:12–17)

Zebulun and Naphtali were Jewish tribes whose region was conquered at the beginning of the Assyrian invasion in 733 BC.

And, as was the case with the appearance of the Magi "from the east" in the infancy narrative, so there are moments in the Galilean mission of Jesus when the reader gets flashes of an expansive future mission to the nations. In Matthew's dramatic opening scene of Jesus's public ministry, crowds stream to Jesus from all the points of the compass, bringing their sick with them: "And great crowds from Galilee, the Decapolis, Jerusalem, and

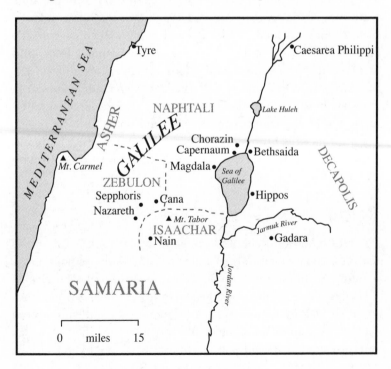

Judea, and from beyond the Jordan followed him" (Matt 4:25) — a multitude that prompts Jesus to proclaim the Sermon on the Mount.

In the course of his Galilean mission, Jesus is confronted by two Gentiles seeking healing whose faith is astounding. The first is the centurion in Capernaum who asks Jesus to heal his servant. Capernaum was a border town between the regions ruled by the sons of Herod, Philip and Herod Antipas; the officer was probably not a Roman soldier but a member of the militia of the region. When Jesus offers to come to the man's home, he protests, "Lord, I am not worthy to have you enter under my roof; only say the word and my servant will be healed" (Matt 8:8). The man's faith seems to catch Jesus by surprise and prompts a glimpse of the future: "Amen, I say to you, in no one in Israel have I found such faith. I say to you, many will come from the east and the west, and will recline with Abraham, Isaac, and Jacob at the banquet in the kingdom of heaven" (Matt 8:10–11). Similarly, in Jesus's encounter with the "Canaanite" woman (a term evoking the traditional enemies of ancient Israel situated along the Mediterranean coast), he at first emphatically rejects her appeal but is ultimately struck by her persevering faith and exclaims, "O woman, great is your faith! Let it be done for you as you wish" (Matt 15:28).

REJECTION IN GALILEAN TOWNS

As in Mark's account, despite the many examples of Jesus's teaching and healing in the Galilee region, Galilee is not seen as a purely positive arena for Jesus's mission. Matthew's Gospel describes the mounting opposition to Jesus by the Jewish leaders who take exception to his healings on the Sabbath, accuse him of being allied with Satan, and object to what they see as lax interpretation of the cultic laws. In Matthew, too, his hometown people of Nazareth do not accept Jesus (13:54–58).

To all of this Matthew adds a lament about the reception Jesus receives in the towns near the northwest corner of the Sea of Galilee:

> Then he began to reproach the towns where most of his mighty deeds had been done, since they had not repented. "Woe to you, Chorazin! Woe to you, Bethsaida! For if the mighty deeds done in your midst had been done in Tyre and Sidon, they would long have repented in sackcloth and ashes. But I tell you, it will be more tolerable for Tyre and Sidon on the day of judgment than for you. And as for you, Capernaum:
>
> 'Will you be exalted to heaven?
>   You will go down to the netherworld.'
>
> For if the mighty deeds done in your midst had been done in Sodom, it would have remained until this day. But I tell you; it will be more tolerable for the land of Sodom on the day of judgment than for you." (Matt 11:20–24)

Here is a prime example where both geography and history overlap to add poignancy and strength to the gospel language.

CONCLUSION

For Matthew, as in Mark, Galilee is the place "where most of [Jesus's] mighty deeds had been done" (Matt 11:20). Here, too, Jesus proves his fidelity to his God-given mission to minister to the "lost sheep of the house of Israel" (10:6). Yet in Matthew's Gospel those "lost sheep" on the perimeter of God's people are also a sign of the many others who "will come from east and the west, and will recline with Abraham, Isaac, and Jacob" (8:11). Yet too in Galilee deadly opposition begins to build against Jesus from the religious authorities, but also from some of the towns in the region who are unresponsive to Jesus's ministry. As in Mark's landscape, the full destiny of Jesus requires the journey from Galilee to Jerusalem.

THE MOUNTAINS

In most traditional cultures mountains have a sacred symbolic meaning as the locus of revelation or contact with the divine. This is certainly true in the Bible, where mountains are mentioned more than five hundred times. In the Book of Exodus, Mount Sinai is the place where Moses sees God "face to face" and is given the gift of the law, sealing Yahweh's covenant with Israel (Exod 19– 20). Mount Zion is the location of Jerusalem and is considered the centerpoint of the earth, and on this sacred mountain the temple would be built (Isa 28:16).

Mountains are especially important in Matthew's Gospel. In Matthew's version of the desert test of Jesus, the final confrontation with Satan takes place on a "very high mountain" where Satan shows Jesus "all the kingdoms of the world in their magnificence" (Matt 4:8), a seduction to power that Jesus rejects.

Even more significant is that Matthew begins the public ministry of Jesus in a mountain setting, a sharp contrast with the inaugural action of Jesus in Mark's narrative, which takes place in the synagogue of Capernaum (Mark 1:21–28). Matthew prefaces Jesus's ascent to the mountain with the dramatic panorama found in 4:23–25. Jesus, Matthew notes, "went around all of Galilee, teaching in their synagogues, proclaiming the gospel of the kingdom, and curing every disease and illness among the people." And streaming toward him come the multitudes of sick and infirm as if drawn by some magnetic power. It is at that moment that Jesus "went up the mountain, and after he had sat down, his disciples came to him" and "he began to teach them" (Matt 5:1–2). What follows is the first and decisive discourse of Jesus in

Matthew's Gospel, the Sermon on the Mount (Matt 5—7), a foundational summary of Jesus's teaching. Given Matthew's strong sensitivity to the Jewish roots of Jesus's mission, it is most likely that the evangelist evokes here the memory of Mount Sinai and the role of Moses as the great lawgiver of God's people.

Other significant mountain top scenes occur in Matthew's narrative. In a passage unique to Matthew's Gospel and one that seems to recapitulate the beginning of the Sermon on the Mount, Jesus ascends a mountain near the Sea of Galilee and sits down. There follows another epic moment that accentuates Jesus's power to heal: "Great crowds came to him, having with them the lame, the blind, the deformed, the mute, and many others. They placed them at his feet, and he cured them. The crowds were amazed when they saw the mute speaking, the deformed made whole, the lame walking, and the blind able to see, and they glorified the God of Israel" (Matt 15:30–31).

At the beginning of the journey of Jesus and his disciples to Jerusalem, Matthew follows the lead of Mark and includes the scene of Jesus's transfiguration on "a high mountain" (Matt 17:1–8). Here again the memory of the theophany at Sinai is evoked, with the presence of Moses and Elijah and the elements of the "bright cloud cast[ing] a shadow over them," and the divine voice speaking from the cloud: "This is my beloved Son, with whom I am well pleased; listen to him." Similar to Mark's account, when Jesus arrives in Jerusalem, he will deliver his apocalyptic discourse (chapters 24—25) on the Mount of Olives, the traditional site associated with the final judgment. And, as we will note below, the conclusion of Matthew's entire narrative takes place on a mountain in Galilee "to which Jesus had ordered them," where the risen Christ will reunite with his disciples after the trauma of the passion and send them out on their mission to the nations (28:16–20).

All these mountain scenes, taking place where heaven and earth meet, highlight the transcendent nature of Jesus: the beloved Son of God, the authentic teacher of Israel, the definitive healer, the source of the community's mission to the world, and the triumphant Son of Man who will gather the nations in judgment at the end of time.

JERUSALEM

For the climactic events that take place in Jerusalem, Matthew closely follows the landscape and sequence of events provided by Mark, with only a few subtle changes or additions.[4] When Jesus is turned over to Pilate by the religious leaders, Matthew adds the incident of Judas's remorse and his attempt to return to the chief priests and elders the thirty pieces of silver he had gained in betraying Jesus (Matt 27:3-10). Rebuffed by the leaders, Judas despairs, casting the blood money into the temple and hanging himself. The leaders take the money and "buy the potter's field as a burial place for foreigners." And Matthew adds, "That is why that field even today is called the Field of Blood"—an incident that the evangelist sees as the fulfillment of Scripture, adapting a quotation from Zechariah 11:12-13 but attributing it to Jeremiah, perhaps to evoke the foreboding tone of this prophet (27:9).

To the dramatic events that break out at the moment of Jesus's death on Golgotha—the tearing of the temple veil and the acclamation of the centurion and his companions (made plural in Matthew)—Matthew adds the earthquake, the splitting of the rocks, and the opening of the tombs of the "many saints," who, after the resurrection of Jesus, "entered the holy city and appeared to many" (27:51-52), a unique scene that seems to fulfill Ezekiel's vision of the dry bones who are liberated from their graves and given flesh and renewed life by the Spirit of God, a sign that God will renew the life of his people (Ezek 37). Again, as in Mark, the passion narrative concludes with the burial of Jesus by Joseph of Arimathea in a "new tomb that he had hewn in the rock" while the faithful women who had stood by the cross witness the event (Matt 27:57-61).

GO TO THE NATIONS

Similar to Mark's account, Matthew first proclaims the resurrection through the discovery of the empty tomb and the testimony of "an angel of the Lord" who roles back the stone from the entrance and announces to the women that Jesus has been raised "just as he said" (28:1–8). This testimony contrasts with the bad faith of the religious leaders who bribe the soldiers guarding the tomb to say that Jesus's disciples had stolen the body (Matt 27:62–66; 28:11–15). Another important addition by Matthew is an appearance of the risen Jesus himself as the women leave the tomb to inform the disciples. The risen Jesus repeats the message of the angel: "Do not be afraid. Go tell my brothers to go to Galilee, and there they will see me" (28:9–10). The command is to return to Galilee, the place where the disciples were first called to follow Jesus and where the mission of Jesus himself would be revealed.

The final scene of the Gospel is unique to Matthew. As noted previously, the risen Christ appears to his "eleven disciples" (continuing Matthew's focus on the loss of Judas) declaring, "All power in heaven and on earth has been given to me. Go, therefore, and make disciples of all nations, baptizing them in the name of the Father, and of the Son, and of the holy Spirit, teaching them to observe all that I have commanded you. And behold, I am with you always, until the end of the age" (28:18–20). With this climactic scene, Matthew extends the landscape of the Gospel out to "to the nations" and extends the presence of the risen Christ with the community "until the end of the age." The mission of Jesus prior to the resurrection had been confined to the land of Israel; now those boundaries fall away, and the arena of the mission is the entire world, still including Israel but also now embracing the Gentiles. At the beginning of the Gospel narrative, the evangelist had turned the readers' attention to Israel's past, beginning with the patriarch Abraham. Now the reader is invited to turn to the "nations" and to the future.

THE LANDSCAPE OF THE GOSPELS

Here again we see that the spiritual landscape fashioned by Matthew amplifies the theological message of his Gospel.

CHAPTER THREE

The Landscape of the Gospel of Luke and the Acts of the Apostles

Geography and its historical and symbolic overlay play a major role in both the Gospel of Luke and the Acts of the Apostles. Luke fuses on to his Gospel narrative a second volume that traces the rapidly expanding horizon of the church's mission. It is more difficult to pinpoint the precise location and specific audience of Luke's work, but its purpose is clear. In his formal prologue the author tells "Theophilus" (the real or fictive reader of Luke's account) that he wishes to confirm for him the reliability of the instruction he has been given by presenting an "orderly sequence" of all that has happened from the beginning until the present moment (Luke 1:1-4). In other words, Luke wishes to paint the big picture of the marvelous works of God—rooted in Judaism, flowering in the mission of the crucified and risen Jesus, and, now, through the power of the Spirit sent by the exalted risen Christ, reaching out from Jerusalem to the "ends of the earth."

Similar to Matthew, Luke's primary sources for his Gospel include the Gospel of Mark and the "Q" source, a collection of Jesus's sayings and parables, along with special material unique to Luke and his community. Mark's general landscape of a desert beginning, followed by the Galilean mission of Jesus, then the journey to Jerusalem, followed by the decisive events of Jesus's final days in Jerusalem is retained by Luke. But he places his own distinctive imprint on this basic landscape.

Identifying the sources Luke uses to compose the Acts of the Apostles is difficult. In some parts of his account, the author uses the first-person plural — "we" — suggesting that he may have accompanied Paul and his other companions during some of his missionary journeys.[1] The author of Acts may also have had contact with at least some of Paul's letters. The evangelist most likely had access to fundamental historical information about most of the events he narrates. At the same time, there is no question that the evangelist arranges his sources and injects his own perspective to offer Theophilus a theological interpretation of the history he narrates.

PART I: THE LANDSCAPE OF THE GOSPEL OF LUKE

ROOTED IN THE HEART OF JUDAISM: JERUSALEM AND ITS TEMPLE

Luke, like Matthew but in a very different fashion, pushes the origin of Jesus back to the time of Jesus's conception and birth. The evangelist anticipates the link between John and Jesus that will take place at Jesus's baptism (3:1–22). Luke portrays in parallel fashion the conception and births of these two figures of destiny through Elizabeth and Zachary and Mary and Joseph — in all instances with Jesus seen as superior to John.

Right from the outset, Luke puts the spotlight on Jerusalem and its temple. The child John is conceived by Elizabeth while Zachary is fulfilling the time of his priestly service in the temple (1:5–25). Meanwhile in "a town of Galilee called Nazareth," the angel Gabriel appears to Mary and announces her virginal conception of Jesus (1:26–38). Luke's account artfully brings Jesus of

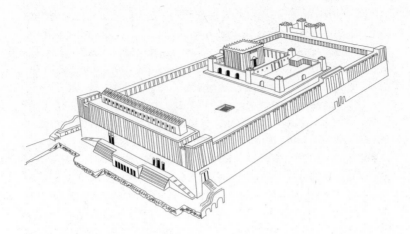

Nazareth and John of Judea together through the visitation of the pregnant Mary to her also pregnant cousin Elizabeth, one of the most beautiful scenes in the New Testament, as the infant John leaps for joy in his mother's womb at the sound of Mary's greeting (1:19–56). Later, Joseph will bring his betrothed from Nazareth (presumably their normal domicile) to his ancestral home of Bethlehem, the city of David, because of the census commanded by Caesar Augustus and enforced by Quirinius the governor of Syria (Luke 2:1–3). Thereby, Luke emphasizes the Davidic descent of Jesus but also signals the wider map of the Roman Empire that will come into play in his second volume.

Luke's focus on Jerusalem and its temple continues in other scenes from his infancy Gospel. After Jesus's birth, Mary and Joseph take him to the temple for the Jewish ritual of purification, required for a mother who has given birth (Lev 12:28). Here in another exquisite Lukan scene, they encounter two prophets, Anna and Simeon, both devout Jews who welcome Jesus as the longed-for salvation of Israel (Luke 2:22–38). Another temple scene takes place when the child Jesus has reached the age of twelve and his parents bring him from Nazareth to Jerusalem "according to festival custom" (Luke 2:41–42). When the parents start their return to Nazareth, they realize Jesus is missing and discover that he had remained in Jerusalem, "in the temple, sitting in the midst of the teachers, listening to them and asking them questions." When his distraught parents confront him, Jesus replies, "Did you not know that I must be in my Father's house?"

Thus, right from the start, Luke uniquely situates Jesus within the framework of strong Jewish piety, fully at home in Jerusalem and its temple. Nowhere in Luke's account is there any hostility on the part of the Jewish characters of these scenes—a marked contrast with Matthew's infancy narrative, which is filled with the threats of Herod and his court as well as that of his son Archelaus, forcing Jesus and his parents into refuge in Egypt and displacement to Nazareth. For Luke, Jesus emerges from the heart of biblical Israel represented in the humble and devout characters of Elizabeth and Zachary, Mary and Joseph, the shepherds, and the prophets Anna and Simeon. The climax of Luke's Gospel narrative will return to this Jerusalem landscape, where there will be the rejection and sufferings leading to the death of Jesus but also the location of the resurrection of Jesus, his appearances to his disciples, his triumphant ascent to his father, and, in the opening scenes of Acts, the place where the Spirit of God will descend on the disciples.

FROM THE DESERT TO GALILEE

As he begins to describe the public ministry of Jesus, Luke follows the basic landscape found in his source, Mark, but expands it. The opening scenes take place in the Judean desert (3:1−4:13), but Luke relates the advent of John—and therefore Jesus—to the wider political, geographical, and religious landscape of the time. He cites the imperial rulers—"In the fifteenth year of the reign of Tiberius Caesar, when Pontius Pilate was governor of Judea"—and their vassals, Herod, the "tetrarch of Galilee" (i.e., Lower Galilee), his brother Philip, "tetrarch of the region of Iturea [north of Galilee] and Trachonitis" (east of the Sea of Galilee),[2] and Lysanias, another Roman-backed ruler whose precise dates are debated and who ruled in the small Syrian region surrounding the city of Abilene, northwest of Damascus. Luke also notes that this was during the "high priesthood of Annas and Caiaphas" (Luke 3:1–2). John's ministry itself is expansive, as he brings his message of repentance and his ministry of baptism "throughout [the] whole region of the Jordan" (3:3).

Beginning in Nazareth

Luke also follows Mark's lead in inaugurating the Galilean ministry of Jesus after the baptism at the Jordan and Satan's test of Jesus in the desert, but here again Luke adds distinctive touches to the landscape. Luke's most dramatic change is to begin Jesus's mission not in the synagogue of Capernaum as in Mark, nor on the Galilean mountaintop as in Matthew, but in the synagogue of Nazareth "where he had grown up" (Luke 4:16–30). Jesus selects the Sabbath Torah reading from Isaiah 61 and its message of justice and liberation that will characterize Jesus's own message in Luke's Gospel:

> The Spirit of the Lord is upon me,
> because he has anointed me
>   to bring glad tidings to the poor.
> He has sent me to proclaim liberty to captives
> and recovery of sight to the blind,
>   to let the oppressed go free,
> and to proclaim a year acceptable to the Lord.

Jesus's hometown audience is, at first, "amazed" by Jesus's compelling eloquence, but the mood turns hostile as Jesus cites the deeds of the great prophets Elijah and Elisha, whose works went beyond the boundaries of ancient Israel. They want Jesus to perform his works of healing in Nazareth ("that we heard were done in Capernaum") and confine his ministry to them ("Surely you will quote me this proverb, 'Physician, heal yourself'"). Jesus instead reminds them that rather than focus exclusively on Israel, Elijah ministered to a widow in Zarepthath, a village in the region of Sidon (1 Kgs 17) and Elisha healed the leprosy of the haughty royal official Namaan, the Syrian (2 Kgs 5). Through these references to Elijah and Elisha, Luke not only brings into view regions beyond Israel — a sign of the universal mission to come — but also wraps Jesus in the mantle of these great prophets of old. Enraged, the townspeople attempt to throw Jesus from "the brow of the hill on which their town had been built" (4:29; in fact, a sharp cliff is found on the outskirts of Nazareth), "but he passed through the midst of them and went away."

This dramatic encounter in Nazareth anticipates the entire mission of Jesus: his work of healing and proclamation, his outreach to those on the margins, the hostility that will lead to his death, and yet Jesus's victorious passage from death to life in his resurrection and ascension. It also lays the foundation for the future universal mission of the community.

The Galilean Ministry of Jesus

The rest of Jesus's ministry in Galilee takes place in the general landscape already established in Mark's narrative — in the towns and villages of the region and around, and on, the Sea of Galilee. Luke, however, will alter some of the sequence of Mark's narrative, adding some incidents unique to his Gospel (e.g., raising the son of the Widow of Nain [7:11–17]; forgiving the woman in the house of Simon the Pharisee [7:36–50]), but also omitting some of Mark's material (such as the healing of the Syro-Phoenician woman, and the second feeding story). As in Mark and Matthew, it is in Galilee that Jesus first gathers his disciples and commissions them to proclaim his message of salvation, with Luke's portrayal of the calling of Simon and his fishing companions done in a unique fashion on the sea itself (see Luke 5:1–11). Luke also notes the impact of Jesus's mission reaching beyond the boundaries of Israel, as in the summary of 6:17–19, where he notes that crowds came to Jesus "from all Judea and Jerusalem and the coastal region of Tyre and Sidon…to hear him and to be healed of their diseases." This summary prefaces the great discourse of Jesus that parallels Matthew's Sermon on the Mount, but, in Luke, the discourse takes place "on a stretch of level ground" (6:17). Similar to Mark's account of the Gadarene demoniac (Mark 5:1–2), Jesus crosses the sea "to the territory of the Gerasenes" (Luke does not refer to the Decapolis, as in Mark) and uses this healing of the demoniac as a sign of the future Gentile mission (see Luke 8:39). Luke retains the story about Jesus's calming of the storm at sea (8:22–25) but does not include Mark's account of the walking on the water.

Beyond Galilee

Overall, the gospel landscape in Galilee retains the same character in Luke as it does in Matthew and Mark. It is here that the dynamic mission of Jesus bursts into view, proclaiming the advent of the kingdom of God and through his healings and exorcisms already bringing that kingdom to reality ("But if it is by the finger of God that [I] drive out demons, then the kingdom of God has come upon you," Luke 11:20). Here, too, the opposition to Jesus by the religious leaders and even by his own townspeople begins to build, anticipating the passion that will come in Jerusalem. Yet Luke's narrative does not focus on Galilee to the same extent as in Mark and Matthew. There is no return to Galilee at the end of Luke's Gospel. As we will note, the focus falls rather on the journey from Galilee to Jerusalem and then the dynamic continuation of that journey from Jerusalem to the "ends of the earth."

THE JOURNEY TO JERUSALEM

Like Mark and Matthew, Luke sets the journey of Jesus and his disciples from Galilee to Jerusalem as the central portion of his overall Gospel narrative. However, Luke gives significantly more emphasis to this journey, underscoring its role as a metaphor for the "journey" of discipleship that is at the heart of Christian life. For Luke, this "journey" brings Jesus not only to Jerusalem but ultimately back to God through the ascension; the Acts of the Apostles also describes the unfolding "journey" of the early Christian church. But in Acts, as we will note, the movement is not from Galilee to Jerusalem but "from Jerusalem to the ends of the earth" (see Acts 1:8). Additionally, in Acts, Luke refers to the early Christian community as the people of the "way" — using the same Greek word, *hodos*, that signifies the way or the journey (Acts 9:2; 18:25; 19:9, 23; 22:4; 24:14, 22).

Luke's focus on the journey of Jesus and his disciples becomes apparent after the scene of Peter's confession of Jesus, which Luke presents not on a high mountain as in Matthew but in a place where "Jesus was praying in solitude" (Luke 9:18), and after the transfiguration (Luke 9:28–36). Luke's narrative marks the beginning of the journey with a formal introduction: "When the days for his being taken up were fulfilled, he resolutely determined to journey to Jerusalem, and he sent messengers ahead of him" (9:51). That journey takes a course not followed in Mark and Matthew when Jesus's messengers enter "a Samaritan village to prepare for his [Jesus's] reception there." The messengers, however, are not welcomed by the Samaritans, since Jesus was on his way to Jerusalem (9:52). Luke's account accurately reflects the historic tension between Samaria and Judea.[3] When the disciples ask Jesus permission "to call down fire from heaven to consume" the Samaritans, Jesus characteristically rebukes the disciples for proposing this type of vengeance. More than once in Luke's account Samaritans are, in fact, presented in a favorable light, as in Jesus's parable of the "Good Samaritan" (10:29–37) and in the account of the healing of ten lepers when only a Samaritan returns to give thanks (17:11–19). Jesus's openness to the Samaritans reflects this Gospel's attentiveness to Jesus's rapport with those on the margins.

The symbolism of the journey to Jerusalem as a metaphor for the experience of Christian discipleship is apparent in the incidents Luke immediately appends to the beginning of the journey. Three sets of would-be disciples come forward with excuses for not immediately following Jesus: one being warned that following the itinerant life of Jesus means having "nowhere to rest [one's] head," and the second asking to defer the journey until he could "go first and bury my father," and the third saying "let me say farewell to my family at home" (Luke 9:57–62). In each instance, the Gospel underscores that the demands of the kingdom of God trump all other responsibilities. The journey continues with Jesus sending out seventy-two disciples ahead of him "to every town and place he intended to visit" (10:1).

Luke continues to refer to Jesus's journey more than in Matthew or Mark. In 13:22, the Gospel notes that Jesus "passed through towns and villages, teaching as he went and making his way to Jerusalem." When some friendly Pharisees warn Jesus that Herod Antipas, the ruler over lower Galilee, wants to kill him, Jesus responds, "Go and tell that fox, 'Behold, I cast out demons and I perform healings today and tomorrow, and on the third day I accomplish my purpose. Yet I must continue on my way today, tomorrow, and the following day, for it is impossible that a prophet should die outside of Jerusalem" (13:32–33). In 14:25, the Gospel notes that "great crowds were traveling with him." And in 17:11, as referenced above, Luke charts Jesus's journey to Jerusalem "through Samaria and Galilee." The final passion prediction is introduced with Jesus's words, "Behold, we are going up to Jerusalem" (18:31). And Luke will chart the final stages of the journey as Jesus "came to Jericho and intended to pass through the town" (19:1). Here the journey is interrupted for Luke's compelling and characteristic story of Jesus's encounter with Zacchaeus, the wealthy tax collector and a man of short stature, whom Jesus befriends and stays at his house—more evidence of this Gospel's focus on Jesus's outreach to those on the margins (see 19:1–10).

Luke's dramatic conclusion to the journey narrative matches the formality of its beginning (see above, 9:51). As in Mark, Jesus's approach to Jerusalem begins with the triumphant entry that is prepared as Jesus arrives at the villages of Bethpage and Bethany on the eastern slope "at the place called the Mount of Olives" (19:28–29, 37). When the triumphant procession crosses the summit, Luke adds Jesus's poignant words over the Holy City: "as he drew near, he saw the city and wept over it" (19:41–44). Luke's story accurately portrays the landscape at this point. From the summit of the Mount of Olives looking west across the Kidron Valley, to this day, one has an overwhelming view of the temple mount (with the magnificent Muslim shrine, the Dome of the Rock, now dominating the scene). The sight provokes Jesus's tears of lament over the city he loves—reflecting the pivotal role Jerusalem has had from the beginning in Luke's narrative: "If this day you only knew what makes for peace—but now it is hidden from your eyes." The journey to Jerusalem is now accomplished and the climax of the Gospel narrative will begin.

FINAL DAYS IN JERUSALEM

Luke's portrayal of the Jerusalem setting for the final days of Jesus's mission is similar to that of his major source Mark.[4] The action moves between Bethany and the Mount of Olives and various settings in Jerusalem and its temple. As Luke notes, "During the day, Jesus was teaching in the temple area, but at night he would leave and stay at the place called the Mount of Olives. And all the people would get up early each morning to listen to him in the temple area" (21:37–38). After some days teaching in the temple area and jousting with the religious leaders (20:1 – 21:4), Jesus predicts the final destruction of the temple and the travails that would face the community in the future—an apocalyptic discourse similar to that of Mark but delivered not on the Mount of Olives but in the temple area itself. The final hours of Jesus's life begin with the Passover in an upper room in the city, move to Jesus's final anguished prayer on "the Mount of Olives" (Luke does not refer to the name Gethsemane), then to "the house of the high priest" for interrogation and a hearing before the entire Sanhedrin (22:39, 54). Jesus is then taken to Pilate for final condemnation, and after a final journey to "the place called the Skull," Jesus is crucified. He was then buried "in a rock-hewn tomb in which no one had yet been buried" (23:33, 53).

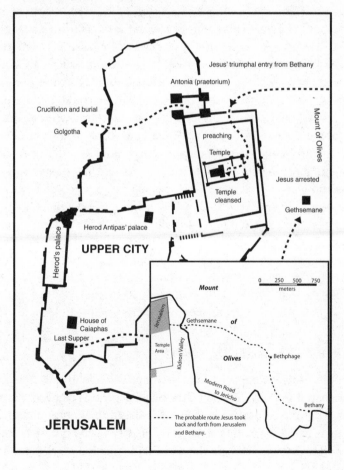

A scene without any parallel in Mark or Matthew is Luke's account of Pilate sending Jesus to Herod Antipas, the ruler of Lower Galilee (23:6–12). Pilate had heard that Herod was in Jerusalem for the feast and, learning that Jesus was a Galilean, and possibly to avoid having to condemn Jesus himself, sent him to Herod since Jesus was under his jurisdiction. Here Luke accurately describes the political situation at the time of Jesus; since the Roman removal of Herod the Great's son Archelaus as ruler of Judea and Samaria in AD 6, Roman prefects ruled directly over this area. But in Lower Galilee, one of Herod the Great's other sons still ruled. Herod Antipas himself is described by Luke as "very glad to see Jesus; he had been wanting to see him for a long time, for he had heard about him and had been hoping to see him perform some sign" (23:8). The reader of Luke's Gospel would not interpret this as sincere curiosity on Herod's part. Earlier, Herod's curiosity about Jesus was linked with his beheading of John the Baptist: "'John I beheaded. Who then is this about whom I hear such things?' And he kept trying to see him" (9:9). Even more ominous was the warning given to Jesus by some Pharisees that "Herod wants to kill you" (13:31–33). When he does encounter Pilate's prisoner, the ruler whom Jesus had called "a fox" (13:32), treats Jesus as a fool and sends him back to Pilate declaring his innocence. Pilate's gesture turns the former enmity between himself and Herod into a friendship—a bond hardly considered positive by the Gospel (23:12). Galilee and Jerusalem are brought together here but by those who are oblivious to the identity of Jesus.

JERUSALEM AND BEYOND

Jerusalem clearly has a more emphatic role in Luke's narrative than it does in the other Synoptic Gospels. The gospel drama had begun in Jerusalem and its temple and the entire mission of Jesus was intentionally oriented to this city of the prophets. And from this city would begin the worldwide mission of the Christian community. All the appearances of the risen Christ will take place, not in Galilee as portrayed in Mark and Matthew, but in and around the Holy City. Luke begins by adding a flair to the account of the discovery of the empty tomb (24:1–12). The faithful women who had stood by the cross come after the Sabbath to anoint Jesus, and there they encounter "two men in dazzling garments" who ask, "Why do you seek the living one among the dead?" To this proclamation of the resurrection, Luke adds that the women report their experience to the "eleven" but are met with skepticism: "but their story seemed like nonsense and they did not believe them" (24:11). Peter, however, runs to the tomb anyway and bends down to peer into the empty tomb, and spotting the burial cloths, he "went home amazed at what had happened" (24:12).

Meanwhile Luke adds the account—unique to his Gospel—of the appearance of the risen Christ to Cleopas and his fellow disciple who leave Jerusalem for the village of Emmaus "seven miles" away, distraught at the death of Jesus. This is one of the New Testament's most beautiful and compelling stories (24:13–35). Here again geography serves Luke's theological purpose.[5] The two despairing disciples are joined by the risen Jesus—invoking the journey that had brought them to Jerusalem in the first place. They are transformed by his explanation of the Scriptures and recognize him in the breaking of the bread. This experience leads them to return to Jerusalem, which is the will of the risen Jesus for his disciples ("And [behold] I am sending the promise of my Father upon you; but stay in the city until you are clothed with power from on high" [24:49]).

When the two disciples rejoin the community in Jerusalem they are told, "The Lord has truly been raised and has appeared to Simon!" (24:34–35). When the two amazed disciples tell of their own encounter, the risen Jesus himself appears again to the entire assembly of disciples (24:36–49). He reassures them it is truly him—the crucified and risen Jesus—by showing them the wounds in his hands and feet and eating a piece of "baked fish." Then, as with the disciples on the road to Emmaus, he "opened their minds to understand the scriptures" and commissions them to be his witnesses to the message of the gospel—a mission in Jesus's name "to all the nations, beginning from Jerusalem" (24:44–49).

The final scene in Luke also embraces the Gospel's spiritual landscape (24:50–53). Jesus "blesse[s] them" and leads them "as far as Bethany" on the eastern slope of the Mount of Olives. Jesus's long earthly journey had begun in Nazareth of Galilee with his conception and then to Bethlehem and Jerusalem for his birth and childhood. In Galilee Jesus's mission would begin to unfold. Now in Jerusalem, the very heart of his Jewish heritage, Jesus's earthly life would reach its final goal—the crucified and risen Jesus is "taken up to heaven," where he would sit in triumph at the right hand of God and send a storm of the Spirit on his beloved disciples. For their part, the disciples offer final homage to Jesus and, as he had instructed them, "returned to Jerusalem with great joy, and they were continually in the temple praising God" (24:52–53).

Thus Jerusalem marks the beginning and the end of Luke's Gospel and dominates its spiritual landscape. The journey of Jesus and his disciples to that Holy City will be recapitulated and transformed by the power of the Spirit, which will lead the followers of Jesus on a journey from Jerusalem to "all the nations" (Luke 24:47), and to "the ends of the earth" (Acts 1:8).

PART II. THE LANDSCAPE OF THE ACTS OF THE APOSTLES

In no other New Testament book does the landscape play a more dominant role than it does in the Acts of the Apostles. The Spirit-driven geographical spread of the early Christian mission "from Jerusalem to the ends of the earth" stands at the heart of Luke's second volume. The overall geographical structure of Acts is paralleled by the two dominant figures of Peter and Paul, with

Peter and his role in the Jerusalem church dominating the first half of the narrative and then giving way to a focus on Paul, who brings the mission to the wider world.

The landscape of Acts is spread over a series of expanding geographical "zones" that dominate the movement of the narrative. Luke first describes the dynamic Jerusalem church and its outreach to the surrounding areas of Judea, Samaria, Gaza, Joppa, and Galilee. Here Peter and the Twelve dominate the narrative. A climactic point takes place in Acts 10:1 – 11:18, when Peter, inspired by the Spirit, accepts the Gentile and Roman officer Cornelius into the community. A second "zone" begins with the missionary journeys of Paul, Barnabas, and John Mark to Cyprus and southern Asia Minor. The figure of Paul and his mission to the west will be the focus — encompassing the territory of Asia Minor, Macedonia, and Achaia. The great apostolic conference at Jerusalem described in Acts 15 gives the seal of approval to this opening to the Gentiles, while respecting the unique role of Jerusalem. A third "zone" begins with Paul's final visit to Jerusalem, leading ultimately to his imprisonment at Caesarea Maritima and his great sea voyage as a prisoner to Rome, the "ends of the earth."

JERUSALEM AND VICINITY

As we have seen in his Gospel, the Jewish roots of Jesus and his mission are a key element of Luke's theological perspective. The focus on Jerusalem — "beginning from Jerusalem" as Luke 24:47 puts it (see also Acts 1:8) — is one important way the evangelist makes this point. The first chapters of the Gospel are set in Jerusalem and its temple, and Jerusalem is also the endpoint of the Gospel narrative. In the opening scenes of Acts, Luke recapitulates the ending of the Gospel, once again addressing Theophilus (as in Luke 1:1–4) and giving more details about the risen Jesus's interaction with his disciples during the "forty days" he was with them before his ascension (Acts 1:1–12).

Luke describes the Jerusalem community in near-ideal terms. Before the storm of Pentecost, the apostles, now joined by Mary, the mother of Jesus, and other women, remain in the "upper room" united in prayer. Guided by Peter, they restore the number of the Twelve—an important link of continuity between the Gospel and Acts—by selecting Matthias to replace Judas. Later, in the famous summaries of the Jerusalem community's life, they will be united in friendship, table fellowship, and common prayer, including daily prayer in the temple (see Acts 2:42–47; 4:32–35). The dominant event, however, is that of Pentecost, when the Spirit promised by the risen Jesus falls upon the community and ignites their apostolic zeal (2:1–41). The scene anticipates the looming universal mission of the community. For the Jewish Feast of Pentecost (the festival that takes place fifty days after Passover), Jews from all over the diaspora ("from every nation under heaven," as Acts 2:5 puts it) converge on Jerusalem and witness this manifestation of the Spirit and hear Peter's discourse. Luke underscores the paradox—these "Galileans" are able, through the power of the Spirit, to be understood by people from virtually all sectors of the biblical compass (see 2:9–11): "Parthians, Medes, and Elamites, inhabitants of Mesopotamia" (traditional peoples from the northeast); "Judea and Cappadocia, Pontus and Asia, Phrygia and Pamphylia" (in addition to Judea, areas of Asia Minor with significant Jewish populations); "Egypt and the districts of Libya near Cyrene" (areas at the other end of the axis with Mesopotamia, including Egypt and parts of Northern Africa); "as well as travelers from Rome" (the imperial capital, whose influence will be noted in various parts of Acts); and finally, seemingly as an afterthought, "Cretans" (the Mediterranean island of Crete) and "Arabs" (the term usually referring to the Nabatean region from Damascus south to Petra in present-day Jordan).

At this point the people mentioned are Jews from Gentile regions. This, too, anticipates the missionary strategy described in Acts, where Paul and his missionary companions go first to their

Jewish compatriots in the synagogue in the places they visit and only afterward reach out to Gentiles, often after being rejected by the majority of the Jews in the synagogue.

Empowered by the Spirit, the gospel starts to be carried by apostolic witness beyond Jerusalem. Luke notes that "a large number of people from the towns in the vicinity of Jerusalem also gathered, bringing the sick and those disturbed by unclear spirits, and they were all cured" (5:16). Paradoxically, the martyrdom of Stephen leads to a persecution of the Jerusalem church and causes members of the community to "scatter...throughout the country-side of Judea and Samaria" (8:1). Among them is Philip, who proclaims the gospel to Samaria (8:4–5; see also 8:25).[6] Later, Philip is instructed by an "angel of the Lord" to go to the road leading from Jerusalem to Gaza, where he encounters the Ethiopian eunuch traveling home, signaling the advent of the gospel into Africa (8:26–39). Luke also portrays Philip going up the Mediterranean coast from present-day Ashdod ("Azotus" is the Greek name for this coastal city) north to Caesarea Maritima, a trip of about sixty miles (Acts 8:40), and infers that the gospel had been taken to Galilee (9:31). And Peter himself will bring the power of teaching and healing to Lydda, a town near the Mediterranean coast (now the sight of Ben Gurion International airport!), and then goes to Joppa, the traditional port city just south of present-day Tel-Aviv, where he cures Tabitha and stays for an extended period in the house of Simon, "a tanner" (9:36–43).

Joppa figures prominently in the Old Testament Book of Jonah as the port from which the prophet attempted to flee from the Lord's command to preach to the Ninevites—one of the Bible's most enticing stories. Can it be that Luke has this in mind in having Joppa be the staging area for Peter's acceptance of the first Gentile convert into the early Christian community? While in Joppa, napping before lunch, Peter has a vision in which he will be summoned to meet Cornelius and his household. This incident is a major turning point in Acts and commands nearly

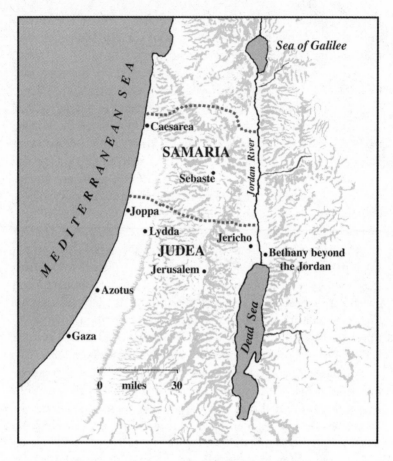

two chapters of the narrative (10:1 – 11:17).[7] Peter is the one whom the Spirit chooses to baptize the first Gentile – a momentous event that will explode into the fullness of the Gentile mission in subsequent chapters of Luke's narrative.

Peter goes to a Roman centurion living in Caesarea Maritima, the seat of Roman power in Judea, where Pilate resided and where later Paul would be imprisoned under the procurators Felix and Festus. Caesarea was also the sea coast portal where Paul and

his companions would move in and out during their missionary journeys to the west (e.g., 21:8) and from which Paul would
be taken on his final journey to Rome (27:1–2). After baptizing
Cornelius and his household, Peter must then return to Jerusalem
to convince his fellow Jewish Christians that the outreach to the
Gentiles is the will of God: "When they heard this [Peter's report],
they stopped objecting and glorified God, saying, 'God has then
granted life-giving repentance to the Gentiles too'" (11:18).

BEYOND JERUSALEM:
ANTIOCH AND POINTS WEST

The next "zone" in the landscape of Acts reaches out into the
wider Mediterranean world, with Antioch as its base.[8] Even prior
to Peter's baptism of Cornelius and his household, this breakout
was anticipated in Luke's account of the conversion of Paul and
its aftermath (9:1–30). On his way to Damascus, Paul, the zealous
persecutor of the Christian community (8:3), encounters the risen
Christ, an experience that will change Paul's life and the course
of Christian history. After being healed by Ananias, Paul immediately begins preaching in Damascus and ultimately has to flee to
Jerusalem where Barnabas introduces him to the apostles. When
Paul stirs up trouble with the "Hellenists" (presumably Greek-
speaking Jews in Jerusalem), he is sent off to sail from Caesarea to
his home base of Tarsus in southern Asia Minor.

The first arrival of the Christian message in Antioch happens,
paradoxically, because of the persecution that breaks out in Judea
in the wake of Stephen's martyrdom (11:19). Here again Luke
tracks the geography: "Now those who had been scattered by the
persecution that arose because of Stephen went as far as Phoenicia
[the present-day Lebanese coast], Cyprus, and Antioch....There
were some Cypriots and Cyrenians [northern Africa] among them,
however, who came to Antioch and began to speak to the Greeks
[i.e., Gentiles] as well, proclaiming the Lord Jesus. The hand of the

Lord was with them and a great number who believed turned to the Lord" (11:19–21). Here is another intriguing motif of Acts — the spread of the gospel is not the result of careful pastoral planning on the part of the apostles but appears, on the human level, to take place haphazardly and unexpectedly. But Luke's theological perspective sees all of this as the inexorable plan of God propelled by the Spirit.

Antioch, named after the Seleucid ruler Antiochos, was the third largest city in the Roman Empire in the first century and a major caravan route and trading center between the Roman Empire to the west and the vast world that stretched east to Mesopotamia and beyond.[9] Archaeology confirms that it also had a significant Jewish population in the first century, a situation accurately reflected in Acts, which will portray Antioch as the bridge between the Jerusalem Jewish-Christian community and the newly formed Gentile communities that would spring up in the wake of the missionary journeys of Paul, Barnabas, and their companions. When word that Gentiles were being baptized in Antioch first comes to the Jerusalem community, they are once again alarmed and send Barnabas to check out the situation. His report (as Peter's had after the baptism of Cornelius) calms the community: "When [Barnabas] arrived and saw the grace of God, he rejoiced and encouraged them all to remain faithful to the Lord in firmness of heart." Acts goes on to praise Barnabas, who apparently played such a pivotal, mediating role in the early church: "For he was a good man, filled with the holy Spirit and faith" (11:23–24).

Continuing this role as a reconciler, Barnabas goes to Tarsus and retrieves Paul, bringing him back to Antioch where they remain for "a whole year" (11:26). In another gesture of reconciliation between Jerusalem and Antioch, the Christians of Antioch send Barnabas and Paul to bring famine relief to the community in Jerusalem (11:27–30; see also 12:25). Luke seems to suggest that it was here in Antioch (where "the disciples were first called Christians," 11:26), that Paul would be more deeply formed in his

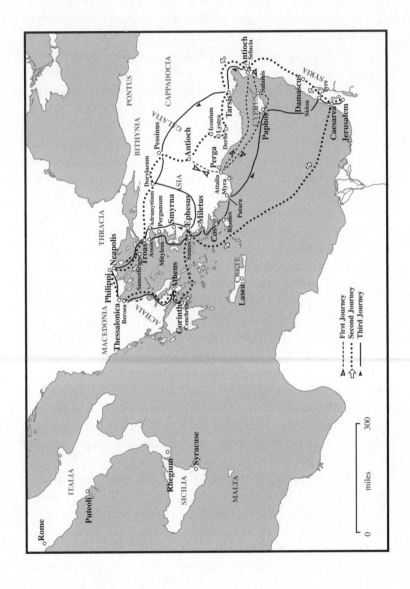

newfound Christian faith and from here that the Christian mission of proclaiming the gospel would be launched west, to Asia Minor and beyond. In the landscape of Acts, Antioch takes its place right after Jerusalem as the providential base for the missionary expansion of early Christianity.

In chapters 13 and 14, Luke describes the first missionary journey of Paul, laying out in some detail the geographical landscape. Paul and Barnabas, now accompanied by John Mark from Jerusalem (see 12:25; 13:5), are inspired by the Holy Spirit to begin (13:1–3). Luke accurately notes that they sailed from Seleucia-in-Pieria, a Hellenistic town that was the seaport of Antioch to the north of the estuary of the river Orontes. Their journey takes them to the main port of Salamis in Cyprus (the island homeland of some of the Christians who first evangelized Antioch; Acts 11:20) and from there they travel overland the length of the island to Paphos, another Cypriot port from which they sail to Perga on the southern coast of Asia Minor. At this point John Mark, for reasons that are not entirely clear, leaves Paul and Barnabas (laying the basis for a later dispute and ultimate separation between the two apostles; see Acts 15:36–41), and they continue inland to Antioch of Pisidia, and then on to the cities of Iconium, Lystra, and Derbe. In a typical pattern that resonates with Luke's theological perspective, the apostles first proclaim the gospel in the local synagogues, often with the result that so-called Gentile "God-fearers" who frequented the synagogues but were not proselytized, would respond favorably while many of the Jews in the congregation would respond with indifference or hostility.

After completing their work in Derbe, the apostles retrace their steps and come back to the region of Pamphylia, but this time sailing from the famous ancient port of Attalia (present-day Antalya), a few miles from their original landfall in Perga. Luke describes their triumphant return: "From there they sailed to Antioch, where they had been commended to the grace of God for the work they had now accomplished. And when they arrived, they called the church together and reported what God had done with them and how he had opened the door of faith to the Gentiles. Then they spent no little time with the disciples" (Acts 14:25–28).

This entire segment of Acts concludes with the formal approbation of the Gentile mission at the great council in Jerusalem (15:1–35). Led by Peter and James, the brother of the Lord, along with Paul and Barnabas, the community recognizes that the mission to the Gentiles is the work of God. At its conclusion, the "apostles and presbyters" send Paul, Barnabas, along with Judas Barsabbas and Silas, with a letter affirming the authenticity of the faith of the Gentile communities in "Antioch, Syria, and Cilicia" — the region covered in the first missionary journey (15:22–35).

THE GOSPEL GOES TO EUROPE

Immediately after the council in Jerusalem, Luke portrays a new phase of Paul's mission. After separating from Barnabas and John Mark (who go to Cyprus), Paul, now with Silas, returns to Asia Minor. At first they revisit the cities in "Syria and Cilicia" that had been the object of their previous journey. Then, guided by the Spirit, they move farther west through the heart of Asia Minor into the regions of Phrygia and Galatia (16:6), toward the western coast of Asia Minor. When they attempt to move farther northwest toward Mysia, "the spirit of Jesus" would not allow them, so they divert to Troas (ancient Troy) on the Aegean coast. There another dramatic turn in the geographical landscape takes place. Paul has a dream in which a "Macedonian" implores him to "come over to Macedonia and help us" (16:9). Now Paul decides to cross the Aegean and bring the gospel to Macedonia, the first footfall of the apostle on what will be European soil: "When [Paul] had seen the vision, we sought passage to Macedonia at once, concluding that God had called us to proclaim the good news to them" (16:10). Luke's knowledge of the landscape is unerring: the missionaries' sea voyage takes them northwest, passing the island

THE LANDSCAPE OF THE GOSPELS

of Samothrace and then landing at Neapolis (present-day Kavala), the port city for Philippi, accurately described as "a leading city in that district of Macedonia and a Roman colony" (16:12).[10]

In Philippi, Paul and his companions will encounter Lydia, a prosperous dealer in "purple goods" and apparently a leader in the Jewish community there, and be offered hospitality in her home (16:13–15).[11] Paul proclaims the gospel in the city and runs into the usual turbulence as a result of his preaching—this time because the effectiveness of Paul's message was competing with the local cults. Finally, they are forced to take leave of Lydia and move farther west into Macedonia. Luke accurately traces their westward journey along what was one of the most well-traveled roads in the Roman Empire, the Via Egnatia, a 528 mile-long highway first constructed in the second century BC that ran from the ancient city of Dyrrhachium (modern Durrës in Albania) through Macedonia to Thessalonica and Thrace, ending in the region of Illyricum on the east coast of the Adriatic. From there voyagers could take a relatively short sea voyage to Italy and on to Rome.

Acts charts Paul's mission through cities along this Macedonian route, from Philippi to Amphipolis and Apollonia, and then to Thessalonica, a major city where, Acts notes, "there was a synagogue." Once again there is the usual pattern of Paul's strategy as presented in Acts: preaching in the synagogue, receiving a mixed reception, but making inroads with Gentile God-fearers (16:2–8). With Paul threatened again, the local Christians send Paul and Silas farther west along the Via Egnatia to Beroea, a city near the site of the ancient capital of Macedonia (17:10–13). When agitators arrive from Thessalonica, Paul must move on again. This time Silas, now joined by Timothy, will stay behind for a while but local Christians escort Paul to the seacoast (the western shore of the Aegean) and then turning south bring him to Athens (whether Paul traveled by ship hugging the coast or by land is not clear).[12]

Paul's great journey concludes with sojourns in two very different Greek cities. Athens, formerly a powerful political capital, was by the time of Paul's visit something of a "university town," still revered for its classical influence on Greek culture but with little commercial or political clout. Luke's description of Paul's stay in Athens, with its agora or marketplace filled with memorials, and the Areopagus, a place for debate and deliberation among the elders of the city, accurately reflects the city's image (17:16–34). Paul's famous speech that begins with the apostle's appeal to the reputation of the Athenians, but ends with a direct proclamation of the gospel, seems to have minimal impact ("When they heard about resurrection of the dead, some began to scoff, but others said, 'We should like to hear you on this some other time.' And so Paul left them" [17:32–33]).

Corinth, the last full stop on Paul's missionary journey, was a very different city: at the time of Paul's visit, it was a robust Roman colony and a thriving commercial center, strategically located on the narrow stretch of land that joins the Peloponnese to the mainland of Greece, roughly halfway between Athens and Sparta. It was served by two ports, Cenchreae on the east and Lechaeum on the west, linked by a road that enabled commercial goods to be transferred from ships unloaded on the Adriatic and then hauled overland to the Aegean, saving the substantial time it would take for ships to sail around the entire southern Pelopennese. Corinth was also the site of the panhellenic or Isthmian athletic games, which drew enormous crowds from all over Achaia and the Peloponnese.[13] Paul was taken under wing by a Jewish-Christian couple, Aquila and Priscilla (affectionately called "Prisca" by Paul in his letters; see Rom 16:3) who, Luke notes, had fled from Rome during the Emperor Claudius's persecution of the Jews (Claudius reigned AD 41–53). Like Paul, they were tentmakers, Acts notes, and Paul stayed with them and plied his trade along with them (18:2–3). The usual pattern of Paul's evangelization took place in Corinth, as it had in so much of his missionary work: proclamation of the gospel in the synagogue of Corinth "every Sabbath," which led to opposition as well as to new converts such as "Crispus, the synagogue official,...along with his entire household" (18:8). Here, too, the agitation Paul's work enkindled would lead to an official complaint brought to Gallio, the proconsul of Achaia.[14]

After "a year and a half" (18:11) stay, Paul would set sail from Corinth's Aegean port of Cenchreae, where there was a Christian community led by "Phoebe, the deacon," a trusted coworker of Paul (see Rom 16:1–2). Paul brought with him Aquila and Priscilla and began the long journey back to Antioch. The travelers stop briefly at the great city of Ephesus, where Aquila and Priscilla would remain, but Paul would continue on to Antioch, with the promise of a later return. Paul's sea route takes him back to the Judean port of Caesarea Maritima and from there he travels overland back to his base in Antioch (18:22).

This momentous journey had taken Paul from Antioch through the heart of Asia Minor and into Macedonia and down the length of Achaia to Corinth, dramatically expanding the landscape of the early community. Several of the cities mentioned in this journey were the recipients of Paul's pastoral letters, beginning with his first letter to the Thessalonians and later correspondence with Philippi, Corinth, and Galatia. While there is little doubt that the content of the speeches given by Paul and other characters in Acts reflects the theological viewpoint of Luke, the geographical framework reveals accurate historical knowledge about the lay of the land through which Paul and his missionary companions traveled. As in the cases of Philippi, Thessaloniki, Athens, and Corinth, for example, the author of Acts not only knows the location of these cities but seems fully aware of their distinctive character.

JERUSALEM AND ROME

Paul's final missionary journey sets the stage for the final dimension of the spiritual landscape not only of the Acts of the

Apostles but of the entire horizon of salvation portrayed by Luke in both of his volumes, the Gospel and Acts.

Luke begins this phase of his narrative in 18:22, noting that after a time Paul again departed from his home base in Antioch "and traveled in orderly sequence through the Galatian country and Phrygia, bringing strength to all the disciples." This new journey would take him to Ephesus, where he rejoins Aquila and Priscilla, and spends considerable time in this great Roman colony (19:1–40). Here, too, Luke reminds us of the gospel's spread to northern Africa (see the incident of the Ethiopian Eunuch in Acts 8:26–40) by introducing Apollos, a zealous Jewish Christian from Alexandria in Egypt (18:24–28). Learning that he knew only about the baptism of John, Aquilla and Priscilla take him aside and "explained to him the Way (of God) more accurately" (18:26). The climax of Paul's stay in Ephesus is the dramatic riot of the silversmiths in the great theatre of Ephesus, stirred up by Paul's effective missionary preaching. At this point, Paul decides to leave Ephesus and revisit the communities he had founded in Macedonia and Achaia, spending "three months" there. Afterward he planned to go to Jerusalem and after that "I must visit Rome also" (19:21) – here Luke signals what will be the finale of Acts.

Finally, Paul sets sail from the port of Philippi, beginning a long and fateful voyage to Caesarea Maritima and on to Jerusalem, one whose route the narrator of Acts describes in great detail (20:1 – 21:14). Paul is accompanied by a significant delegation from communities he had evangelized: Sopater from Boerea; Aristarchus and Secundus from Thessaloniki; Gaius from Derbe; Timothy, Tychicus, and Trophimus from Asia – and apparently Luke himself, who uses "we" throughout this portion of Acts. Paul and his companions first land back at Troas (the port from which Paul had first sailed to Macedonia, see 16:11); here he revives a young man, Eutychus, who had fallen asleep during Paul's long discourse and tumbled out of a window to the ground (20:7–12)! While his companions sail by ship, Paul travels overland to the city of Assos on the west coast of present-day Turkey. The course of the ship is meticulously noted: Mitylene, Chios, Samos, and Miletus. Paul had decided to bypass Ephesus because "he was hurrying to be in Jerusalem, if at all possible, for the day of Pentecost" (20:16). But, sensing that he was facing his final destiny, Paul sent for the elders of the church at Ephesus to come to Miletus (farther south from Ephesus on the Aegean coast) so that he could bid them farewell. What follows is one of the most poignant passages in Acts, as Paul takes leave from his beloved Christians (see 20:17–38). At the conclusion Luke notes, "When he had finished speaking he knelt down and prayed with them all. There were all weeping loudly as they threw their arms around Paul and kissed him, for they were deeply distressed that he had said that they would never see his face again. Then they escorted him to the ship" (20:36–38).

Once again, the narrator of Acts accurately tracks the route taken by Paul and his companions (21:1–8): sailing close to a series of Greek islands, from Miletus to Cos, then the next day to Rhodes and then to Patera, a port on the southwestern coast of present-day Turkey. There they transfer to a ship capable of making the crossing of the open sea to Phoenicia (present-day Lebanese coast). They pass near Cyprus but do not land and then sail on to the port of Tyre. While the ship unloads its cargo, Paul and his companions visit with Christians there who warn Paul not to proceed to Jerusalem. But reboarding the ship, Paul and his companions continue their voyage, stopping at Ptolemais for a day, a port south of Tyre, where they also greet the local Christians, and afterward finally arrive at Caesarea Maritima.

JERUSALEM, CAESAREA MARITIMA, AND ROME: THE FINAL JOURNEY

The final phase of Luke's narrative, chapters 21 – 28, puts into play the full symbolic dimensions of the landscape of Acts. Paul will arrive in Caesarea Maritima, the harbor city that was the

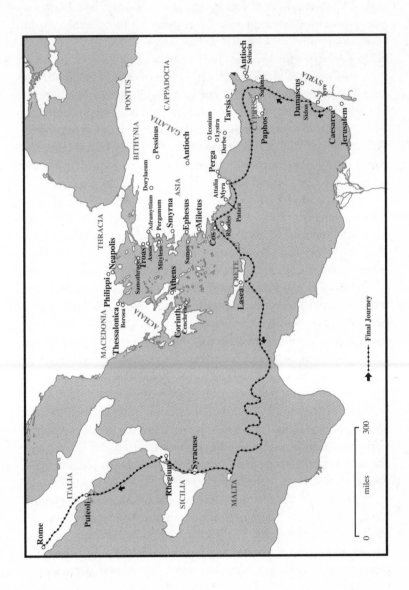

seat of Roman power in Judea, and the portal through the apostolic missionaries would reach out to the wider Gentile world; here, too, Paul would spend the last two years of his life prior to his final journey to "the ends of the earth."

In Caesarea Maritima, there is a replay of what had happened at Miletus and Tyre—Paul's fellow Christians beg him not to go to Jerusalem for fear he will meet deadly opposition. But Paul, like his master before him, is determined to go to Jerusalem: "What are you doing, weeping and breaking my heart? I am prepared not only to be bound but even to die in Jerusalem for the name of the Lord Jesus" (21:13).

Their concern about Paul's fate becomes true. He is welcomed warmly by the Christian community of Jerusalem but his Jewish enemies "from the province of Asia" threaten to kill Paul when he visits the temple. The commander of the Roman cohort rescues Paul and, in a series of dramatic encounters, Acts put on display the full range of Paul's missionary identity—one who can speak Hebrew to the rioters and Greek to the Romans as he reveals his identity as an apostle of Jesus (21:37–40). The commander also learns from Paul that he is a Roman citizen: "I am a Jew, of Tarsus in Cilicia, a citizen of no mean city" (21:39). The crowd's opposition to Paul grows so intense that the Roman soldiers intervene and put Paul under protective custody (23:10). But while in prison, the Lord appears to Paul and assures him once again that God's plan of salvation and the bringing of the gospel to the ends of the earth would not be thwarted: "Take courage. For just as you have borne witness to my cause in Jerusalem, so you must also bear witness in Rome" (23:11).

The rest of the narrative illustrates how that promise is fulfilled, yet in an unanticipated way, as so much of the Spirit-driven events of Acts have been. The Roman commander orders "seventy horsemen and two hundred auxiliaries" to take Paul to Caesarea. Once again, the geographical knowledge of Acts is uncanny; on the way to the coast they stay overnight at Antipatris (present-day Petah Tikva), the sight of abundant natural springs where the horses could draw water during the journey. When Paul arrives in Caesarea, he is placed in custody "in Herod's praetorium" (23:35; Herod the Great had built Caesarea Maritima in honor of his patron, Caesar Augustus). Here he would remain for two years, undergoing interrogations by two successive Roman governors, Felix and Porcius Festus, as well as having visits by King Herod Agrippa and his consort Bernice, who listen to Paul and, along with Festus, are almost convinced to become Christian themselves! Both Agrippa and Festus agree Paul is innocent, but Paul has appealed to Caesar, his right as a Roman citizen (26:30–32). Festus responds, "You have appealed to Caesar. To Caesar you will go" (25:12).

As was the case with Paul's previous sea voyages, the narrator of Acts describes this final sea journey with amazing detail and accuracy (27:1 – 28:14). The first part of the voyage retraces the general route Paul had sailed from Miletus to Caesarea (see above, 21:1–8). Paul and his guard, a centurion named "Julius of the Cohort Augusta," and two companions of Paul, apparently the narrator, along with Aristarchus, a "Macedonian from Thessalonica" and some other prisoners, board a ship that had come to Caesarea from Adramyttium (an ancient seaport on the Aegean coast some seventy miles north of the present-day Turkish city Izmir – that is, ancient Smyrna) that was bound for several ports in Asia Minor. Paul's centurion guard allows him to visit with fellow Christians in Sidon enroute. From there they sail around the northern side of Cyprus (to avoid the headwinds) and reach the port of Myra, on the southwestern coast of Asia Minor.

At this point the centurion arranges for Paul and his companions to transfer to a ship from Alexandria that was bound for Italy. Here trouble begins. Paul warns the centurion about attempting to sail in the open sea since winter was approaching, but the centurion listens to the pilot and they embark on a fateful journey. The pilot hoped to reach a suitable harbor in Crete when they were hit with a powerful storm that pulls the ship off course and into the open sea.

Luke's description of the measures taken to secure the ship are amazing in its detail and knowledge of seafaring. Battered by the storm and facing disaster, the crew jettisons their cargo and even the tackle from the ship. With everyone near despair, Paul recounts a dream he had:

> I urge you now to keep up your courage; not one of you will be lost, only the ship. For last night an angel of God to whom (I) belong and whom I serve stood by me and said, "Do not be afraid, Paul. You are destined to stand before Caesar; and behold, for your sake, God has granted safety to all who are sailing with you." Therefore, keep up your courage, men; I trust in God that it will turn out as I have been told. We are destined to run aground on some island. (27:22–26)

Bringing the gospel to Rome will not be thwarted.

After two weeks adrift, the boat is driven ashore on the island of Malta (27:33 – 28:10), an "accident" that will bring the gospel to a new place. In a gesture reminiscent of his master Jesus, Paul breaks bread with his companions on the ship as it is about to run aground, and "they were all encouraged." Once again Luke demonstrates that the power of God will bring Paul and his gospel message to its goal no matter the obstacles. Several near tragedies happen in succession. When the ship runs aground and breaks up, the soldiers intend to kill the prisoners so they cannot escape, but the centurion wants to save Paul and restrains them. When they get ashore and Paul gathers wood for a fire, he is bitten by a viper but shakes it off and is unharmed. Paul continues his witness to the healing power of Jesus, curing the father of Publius, the "chief of the island," and "the rest of the sick on the island came to Paul and were cured" (28:7–10).

After three days, the amazed survivors set sail for the final stretch, this time on another ship from Alexandria, sailing along the eastern coast of Sicily, stopping at Syracuse and then to Rhegium (present-day Reggio Calabria on the southern tip of Italy across from Sicily), and, finally, with the help of a south wind, they land at the port of Puteoli, near present-day Naples. Paul is greeted by Christians there and after staying awhile, Luke notes almost laconically, "And thus we came to Rome" (28:14).

Acts concludes with a description of Paul continuing his apostolic witness in the heart of the empire, preaching in his usual pattern to the Jews of the area — convincing some and opposed by others (28:17–28). The refusal of Paul's fellow Jews to accept the gospel leads paradoxically to the gospel's universal outreach: "Let it be known to you that this salvation of God has been sent to the Gentiles; they will listen" (28:28) — a quote that recalls the words of Isaiah (40:5) cited at the beginning of the mission of Jesus: "and all flesh shall see the salvation of God" (Luke 3:6).

Luke brings his two-volume work to a close but not to an "ending." Paul, he notes, "remained for two full years in his lodgings [i.e., his house arrest]. He received all who came to him, and with complete assurance and without hindrance he proclaimed the kingdom of God and taught about the Lord Jesus" (Acts 28:30–31). The long journey that had led from Jerusalem to the ends of the earth would now continue through Paul, and beyond his lifetime, through the Christian community.

CONCLUSION

Luke's two-volume work clearly demonstrates the role that the geographical landscape plays in amplifying the evangelist's theological perspective. The landscape of the Gospel brings Jesus, born out of the heart of God's people, the Jews, to Jerusalem and its holy temple. There Jesus would experience death, resurrection, and a triumphant return to God. That journey brought

Jesus's work of proclaiming the kingdom of God from Galilee, through Samaria, and into Judea, where the climax of the Gospel takes place. Through the power of the Spirit, the same Spirit that had descended on Jesus at his baptism and was affirmed at the beginning of his mission in the synagogue of Nazareth, would now fall upon the apostles in Jerusalem and embolden them to be witnesses of the gospel through Judea, Samaria, and to the ends of the earth. Luke's second volume propels the journey of the community out into the Roman Empire—from Antioch to Asia Minor to Macedonia and Achaia. The power of the Spirt sent by Jesus will bring the gospel to "all flesh" no matter the circumstances of opposition, persecution, imprisonment, or even the hostile power of nature. That power of God revealed in Jesus and his mission commands ultimate allegiance that far eclipses any allegiance owed to imperial authority. God's embrace of the world through Jesus knows no bounds.

CHAPTER FOUR

The Landscape of the Gospel of John

In all things, including its "landscape," the Gospel of John has a distinctive character. Despite what seems to be its more abstract portrayal of Jesus, the Fourth Gospel shows deep acquaintance with Jewish symbols and Jewish liturgy and reflects knowledge of the topography of Jerusalem and of the Holy Land in general.[1] While there are general similarities with the framework of the other Gospels — for example, Jesus exercises his public ministry in Galilee and it reaches its climax in Jerusalem and Judea — John's account, in effect, deconstructs the basic geographical framework established by Mark's Gospel and absorbed by both Matthew and Luke. As we have seen, the Synoptic Gospels portray a one-year public ministry of Jesus centered in Galilee, followed by a singular journey to Jerusalem, and concluding with Jesus's final days in the temple, climaxing in the passion and resurrection accounts. John seems to extend Jesus's mission over three years, and Jesus shuttles back and forth between Jerusalem and Galilee. John also accentuates a unique cosmic, spatial framework for Jesus and his mission quite different from that of the Synoptics.

THE COSMIC LANDSCAPE OF JOHN

Each of the Gospels portrays transcendent dimensions of Jesus in their narratives. At Jesus's baptism, the heavens open, the

Spirit descends on Jesus, and the voice of God declares Jesus to be his "beloved son." On a mountaintop in Galilee, Jesus is transfigured in view of his select disciples, accompanied by Moses and Elijah, and his unique status as God's Son is once more affirmed by a heavenly voice. The Synoptic Jesus walks on the water and calms the storm, along with performing a host of healings, including raising the dead. In Luke, the risen Christ ascends to heaven, and in Matthew's account the exalted and risen Christ appears to the women at the tomb and to the eleven apostles on a hilltop in Galilee. Yet John's Gospel adds a "spatial" and cosmic dimension to the gospel framework that is unparalleled in the Synoptic narratives. This cosmic dimension appears in the opening verses of John's account and will be part of the dramatic climax of the narrative. In between there are multiple reference to Jesus's otherworldly origin and his return to the heavenly realm.

John's Gospel begins with a prologue that in poetic terms portrays Jesus's origin in the heavenly realm as the Word who was "with God" before the beginning of time and "was God" (1:1). From this origin in the very inner life of God, the Word descends into the earthly realm, setting the pattern for all of creation, entering into the "world" (i.e., the human realm), which is also made in the pattern of the Word, and ultimately "[becoming] flesh" (1:14).[2] This poetic reflection on the origin of the Word sets a fundamental pattern for the whole of John's Gospel and is the key to much of its theology. Made visible by "becoming flesh" — that is, becoming authentically and fully human — the divine origin of Jesus, his "glory" in Johannine terms, is now recognizable by the Johannine community:

> We saw his glory,
> the glory as of the Father's only Son,
> full of grace and truth. (1:14)[3]

The Prologue concludes with the central christological affirmation of John's Gospel, namely, Jesus's role as the definitive revealer of God: "No one has ever seen God. The only Son, God, who is at the Father's side, has revealed him (1:18).

Thus, the Johannine Jesus is the unique revealer of God, a revelation that will be amplified in the body of John's narrative through the words and deeds of Jesus (the latter designated as "signs," John's term for the miracles of Jesus). The Gospel's first discourse makes explicit the content of that revelation — the essential message that the Word is to communicate to the world: "For God so loved the world that he gave his only Son, so that everyone who believes in him might not perish but might have eternal life. For God did not send his Son into the world to condemn the world, but that the world might be saved through him" (3:16–17).

This function of Jesus as the Word uttered by God and embodying God is affirmed throughout John's narrative by reference to Jesus's heavenly origin, and to both his "descent" and "ascent" between the heavenly realm (i.e., God's presence) and the human realm. This is stated explicitly in Jesus's words to Nicodemus: "No one has gone up to heaven except the one who has come down from heaven, the Son of Man" (3:13). In challenging his disciples in the wake of the Bread of Life discourse, Jesus asks, "What if you were to see the Son of Man ascending to where he was before?" (6:62). When Mary Magdalene encounters the risen Christ in the garden, he tells her not to grasp him: "Stop holding on to me, for I have not yet ascended to the Father" (20:17). Other sets of spatial language in John convey the same idea. Jesus is described as "from above" while his opponents are "from below" or that Jesus does "not belong to this world" (e.g., 8:23; similarly, Jesus's words to Pilate in 19:11).

John's emphasis on the origin of Jesus with God and his descent into the world and becoming "flesh" is matched by an emphasis on Jesus's return to his cosmic origin at the climax of the Gospel. This is explicitly stated in the final words of Jesus to his disciples in the uniquely Johannine final discourse of Jesus in chapter 13—17. While the passion narrative (chs. 18—19) and the resurrection appearances (chs. 20, 21) illustrate the saving impact of Jesus death and resurrection, the meaning of these events is stated in Johannine terms in the final discourse. There Jesus will repeatedly speak of "returning to his Father" and the completion of his mission to reveal God's love for the world (13:1). Jesus goes to "prepare a place" for his disciples in his Father's house (14:1-3). He will not leave them orphans but will send the Paraclete, the Spirit from the heavenly realm where he will go (14:18, 26). Jesus plainly states, "I came from the Father and have come into the world. Now I am leaving the world and going back to the Father" (16:28).

Jesus's words of return to the Father intensify in chapter 17 (vv. 11, 13) and take the form of a prayer for his disciples who remain in the world, as well as for those who will encounter God's word through them. The disciples of Jesus are "sent" into the world just as Jesus himself was sent—so they, too, are to reveal God's love for the world through their witness of self-transcendent love and through loving service (see 13:14, 35; see also the same mission formula in 20:21).

Through this use of such spatial or "cosmic" categories, John's Gospel does not intend to portray Christian life and the Christian mission as somehow disassociated from the hopes and sufferings of the human realm. Rather, by emphasizing the heavenly origin and destiny of Jesus, the Word made flesh, John underscores the astounding fact that the transcendent God of the universe has both created and intensely loves the world and its human inhabitants. The destiny of this world is not condemnation but salvation and a future in which all of humanity will be bound to God in eternal love and life, just as Jesus and the Father are bound together in unfathomable love (17:26).

THE TESTIMONY OF JOHN THE BAPTIST

If John's Gospel frames the beginning and end of the story of Jesus and his mission with a spatial or cosmic dimension, the narrative in between stands on the familiar terrain of the earthly biblical landscape. As in the Synoptics, John the Baptist dominates the opening scenes of John's narrative. At the very outset of his ministry, like Israel of old, Jesus's mission begins in the desert, but the fidelity of Jesus to his mission is in obvious contrast with the failings of ancient Israel in its desert sojourn. In John's Gospel, however, a desert setting for John the Baptist's ministry is only hinted at in the quotation from Isaiah: "I am 'the voice of one crying out in the desert'" (John 1:23). There is no mention of Jesus's baptism nor is there any satanic test of Jesus. Instead John's Gospel underscores the testimony of the Baptist about Jesus—a witness role first cited in the Prologue: "[John] came for testimony, to testify to the light, so that all might believe through him. He was not the light, but came to testify to the light" (1:7–8). This subordinate testimonial role for John is emphasized again in John 1:19–28 and 1:29–34, to be picked up again in 3:22–30.

The only geographical reference provided is the information that John was baptizing "in Bethany across the Jordan" (John 1:28). The exact location of this "Bethany"—no doubt so named to distinguish it from the Bethany on the Mount of Olives (see 11:1; 12:1)—is uncertain. Some ancient manuscripts refer instead to "Bethabara," the name for the baptismal site that is found on the sixth-century AD Madaba map of the Holy Land and also cited by Origen and John Chrysostom.[4] Its precise location is also uncertain, although John's Gospel situates it on the east side of the Jordan river and within relatively easy travel distance for the Jerusalem "priests and Levites" who come to question John (see 1:19). Later, Jesus will take refuge at this place when the Jerusalem authorities attempt to arrest him (10:40). In John's account, the

Baptist himself seems to have something of an itinerant ministry; in 3:23 he performs baptisms in "Aenon near Salim, because there was an abundance of water there"—another site whose precise location is uncertain. Since John's disciples refer to the original place where he encountered Jesus as "across the Jordan" (3:26), that is, on the east side, we can presume that Aenon (which means "springs") is on the west side. The Madaba map places it near Jericho.

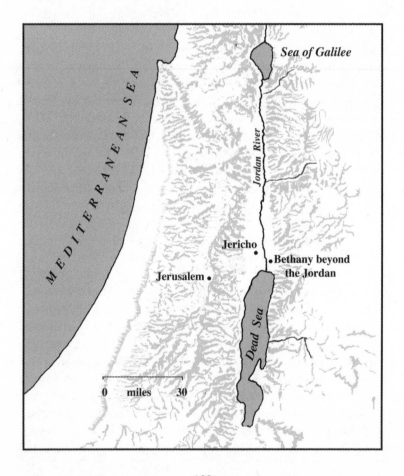

John's high Christology is at work in the opening scenes of his Gospel. Jesus does not submit to baptism by John, and John's sole role is to testify to the exalted identity of Jesus. John's testimonial that Jesus is the "Lamb of God" (1:29, 36), and the magnetic power of Jesus himself, draw disciples away from the circle of John and lead them to follow Jesus (1:35–42). Nor does Satan have any opportunity to "test" Jesus; Jesus's role as the Word made flesh and the one sent from the Father to redeem the world is evident. By downplaying the desert as the traditional arena of Israel's test, the opening scenes of John's Gospel move in a different direction from its Synoptic counterparts. There is no need for a heavenly voice to acclaim Jesus as "my beloved Son" (see Mark 1:11 and par.); the Prologue of John has already made clear Jesus's intimacy with God and his divine mission.

THE ROLE OF GALILEE IN JOHN'S ACCOUNT

On the third "day" of his public ministry as portrayed by John, Jesus decides to go to Galilee where he will draw to himself the disciples Philip and Nathaniel, both of whom are from the fishing village of Bethsaida on the northern rim of the Sea of Galilee (1:43–51). Mark's Gospel, followed by Matthew and Luke, underscore the dramatic importance of this entry into what will be the zone where most of Jesus's public ministry will take place.[5] John's Gospel, however, does not highlight Jesus's entry into Galilee nor does this region, while still of some importance in John's narrative, serve as the prime locus of Jesus's ministry. Only by the insinuation of his opponents do we learn that Jesus was born in Bethlehem (7:42), and Philip declares to Nathanael that Jesus is the "son of Joseph, from Nazareth" (1:45), earning the scornful comment of Nathanael, "Can anything good come from Nazareth?" (1:46). Otherwise these places are not given any attention in John's Gospel.

Jesus moves back and forth between Galilee and Jerusalem throughout John's narrative, with the majority of Jesus's discourses and signs taking place in Jerusalem and the nearby village of Bethany.[6] At least two times Jesus goes to Jerusalem for the Passover (2:13; 12:1) and for other Jewish festivals (5:1, an unnamed "feast of the Jews," possibly Pentecost; 7:10, Tabernacles or the Feast of Booths; 10:22, Dedication or Hanukkah). Reference to an additional Passover in John 6:4 implies that Jesus's public ministry extended for three years, compared with one year apparently portrayed in the Synoptics. Additionally, John's Gospel portrays Jesus as fleeing from the threats of the Jewish leaders in Jerusalem and Judea and more than once taking refuge in Galilee. Thus the Galilee-Jerusalem axis that forms the backbone of the Synoptic narrative has its place in John's Gospel but plays out differently. Jesus meets strong and deadly hostility in Jerusalem and finds respite in Galilee or other locations.

Some significant events of Jesus's public ministry do take place in Galilee, however. The village of Cana, located in the Jezreel valley between Nazareth and Capernaum, is not mentioned in the Synoptics but is the locus of two miracles of Jesus in John's account.[7] The miracle of changing water into wine at the wedding feast of Cana is the first of Jesus's "signs" — the characteristic Johannine term for Jesus's miracles (2:1–11). After a sojourn in Jerusalem (2:11 – 4:3) and Samaria (4:4–42), Jesus returns to Cana to perform the second of his signs, the healing at a distance of the son of a royal official from Capernaum (4:46–54). While Capernaum is identified as the home base for Jesus's Galilean ministry in the Synoptic Gospels (see, e.g., Mark 2:1, which refers to Capernaum as Jesus's "home"), John's Gospel makes only passing references to Capernaum (see 2:12; 4:46; 6:17; 6:24; 6:59). That Jesus along with his mother and disciples "go down" to Capernaum after the wedding feast at Cana (2:12) and the fact that the crowds look for him in Capernaum (6:24), in whose synagogue he delivers the Bread of Life discourse (6:59), suggest that this was a familiar locus for Jesus. Note that embedded in John's accounts of both the wedding feast of Cana and the healing of the official's son is an accurate awareness of the topography; both texts speak of "going down" to Capernaum (2:12 and 4:49), reflecting the fact that Capernaum, although to the northeast of Cana, is 686 feet below sea level (in fact, the lowest freshwater lake in the world) and thus "down" from Cana.

Other events take place in Galilee as well, most notably the sequence that consumes chapter 6 of John's narrative. At the conclusion of chapter 5 Jesus is in Jerusalem, jousting with the "Jews" in the wake of his Sabbath healing of the paralyzed man at the pool of Bethesda (5:1–47). Abruptly, John places Jesus back in Galilee, crossing the Sea of Galilee (6:1). Note that while the Synoptic Gospels refer to the "sea" numerous times, John presents Jesus around and on the sea only in chapter 6 and in the extended ending of his Gospel in chapter 21. John adds the designation "...of Tiberias," which may be a later gloss on the text (see also 21:1). The city of Tiberias was founded by Herod Antipas around AD 20, as a tribute to his patron the emperor, and gradually eclipsed Sepphoris in western Galilee as the leading city of the region of Lower Galilee. There is no Gospel account of Jesus's visiting Tiberias (or Sepphoris). John, however, besides referring to the Sea of Tiberias, notes that crowds came by boat from Tiberias to seek Jesus after the multiplication of the loaves (6:23).

John's sequence of the multiplication of the loaves (6:1–15) followed by the walking on the sea (6:16–21) finds a parallel in Mark 6:34–52.[8] Yet there are subtle differences in these accounts of the multiplication, most notably is John's attention to the reaction of the crowds who, having witnessed the miracle of the loaves, acclaim Jesus as "truly the Prophet, the one who is to come into the world" and then try to make him king (6:14–15)—both inadequate responses to Jesus's signs from the point of view of John's Gospel. Consequently, Jesus withdraws to "the mountain alone" (6:15)—setting the stage for the miracle of the walking on the water. John will revert to the crowd's reaction in the passage that follows the walking on the water (6:22–26). Crowds eagerly seeking Jesus converge on Capernaum, but Jesus himself is wary of their response: "Amen, amen I say to you, you are looking for me not because you saw signs but because you ate the loaves and were filled" (6:26).

The superficial faith of the crowds—not truly "seeing" the signs but only interested in the surface result of abundant bread—leads into the Bread of Life discourse, which consumes the rest of chapter 6. There Jesus will use the metaphor of the "living bread" that came down from heaven as a symbol of his own body and blood—that is, his very presence as the Word made Flesh—and the faith in Jesus this requires. John 6:51—"the bread that I will give is my flesh for the life of the world"—reflects the words of the institution accounts in the Synoptics and suggests a connection to the Christian experience of the Eucharist.

With this scene, John concludes his account of Jesus's work in Galilee. The Gospel notes that after the discourse in Capernaum, "Jesus moved about within Galilee; but he did not wish to travel in Judea, because the Jews were trying to kill him" (7:1), emphasizing again that Galilee was a place of refuge for Jesus. Yet after Jesus stays on in Galilee, he decides to go to Jerusalem "in secret" because the authorities were looking for him (7:9–14).

Thus Galilee plays a significant if muted role in John's narrative. It is the place where Jesus's first signs are manifest, at the wedding feast of Cana and in the healing of the royal official's son. And here Jesus will multiply the loaves and walk on the water—all dramatic revelations of his divine power, as well as Jesus's care for both the crowds and his disciples. In the Bread of Life discourse presented in the synagogue of Capernaum, Jesus again reveals his salvific mission to "feed" the world with the bread "from heaven" that "gives life to the world" (6:33). Nazareth plays no role except for the disparaging remark of Nathanael, "Can anything good come from Nazareth?" (1:46); nor are other towns of the region mentioned such as Korazim, or Naim, or Tyre and Sidon, or Gerasa, or the Decapolis. For John, the ultimate arena of Jesus's mission is Jerusalem.

SAMARIA

The ambivalent role of Samaria reflected in the Synoptic Gospels also appears in John's account. The negative view of Samaritans held by Jews is cited in a sharply polemical scene in John 8:48, where Jesus's opponents caustically insult Jesus: "Are we not right in saying that you are a Samaritan and are possessed?" But the Fourth Gospel's extended account of Jesus and the Samaritans occurs in chapter 4, a scene unique to this Gospel, one wrapped in both the geography and history of this region.

John sets the scene as Jesus travels from Jerusalem to Galilee after completing the first major discourse of the Gospel in Jesus's encounter with Nicodemus (3:1–21). John curiously notes that Jesus "had to pass through Samaria" (4:4), but, in fact, there were alternate routes to Galilee, along the Jordan valley or even along the seacoast. Perhaps the "necessity" stated here has to do not with travel routes but with the providential significance of Jesus's mission to these outsiders so early in his ministry. He and his disciples enter the Samaritan town of Sychar, "near the plot of land that Jacob had given to his son Joseph" (4:5; see Gen 48:22; Josh 24:32). These Old Testament texts mention the patriarch's donation of the land to Joseph near Shechem, but there is no reference to "Jacob's well." Venerable Jewish, Christian, and Muslim traditions identify the still-operational well in a village outside of present-day Nablus (the site of ancient Shechem) as "Jacob's well."

While his disciples go into the village to procure something to eat (explained later in the story, 4:27–33), Jesus, exhausted from his journey, sits down at the well to rest. John notes, "It was about noon" (4:6). And there Jesus will encounter an unnamed Samaritan woman who comes to the well by herself to draw water.[9] The

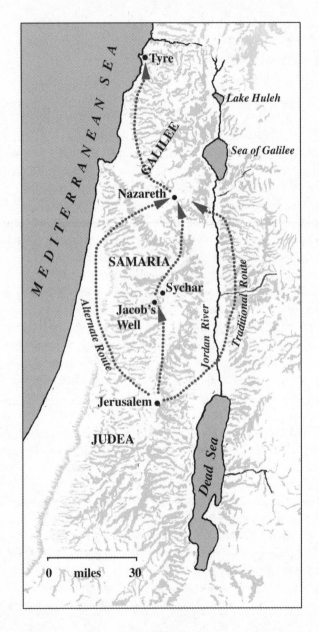

interaction between Jesus and the woman is one of the Gospel's most intriguing passages, leading ultimately to the woman's faith in Jesus and her proclamation of his messianic identity to her villagers: "Many of the Samaritans of that town began to believe in [Jesus] because of the word of the woman who testified, 'He told me everything I have done.'" (4:39). The Samaritans invite Jesus to stay with them, and after his two-day visit, "Many more began to believe in him because of *his* word, and they said to the woman, 'We no longer believe because of your word; for we have heard for ourselves, and we know that this is truly the savior of the world" (4:41–42, author's emphasis). This sequence is typically Johannine—the initial fascination of the woman with Jesus leads to her testimony to others, which in turn brings them in direct contact with Jesus. In many ways, this replicates the sequence of the gathering of Jesus's initial disciples in 1:35–51, where disciples advance from an encounter with Jesus to draw others to him.

Both Jesus and the woman refer to the troubled history between Samaria and Jerusalem. The woman questions why a Jew would ask a Samaritan woman for a drink, with the narrator explaining ("For Jews use nothing in common with Samaritans," 4:9). Jesus's declaration that he can give her "living water" leads to her assertion that the patriarch Jacob had given "us" this well. When the conversation advances and Jesus reveals he knows her troubled marital status, she counters by asserting that her ancestors "worshiped on this mountain" (i.e., Mount Gerizim) and not as the Jews do in Jerusalem. The conversation reaches a climactic point with Jesus declaring the superiority of the Jewish belief over that of the Samaritans ("You people worship what you do not understand; we worship what we understand, because salvation is from the Jews," 4:22). But now the hour has come when "true worshipers will worship the Father in Spirit and truth" (4:23)—leading Jesus to boldly declare to the woman who awaits the coming of the Messiah, "I am he, the one who is speaking with you" (4:26).

This Johannine passage is a prime example of how geography and history illumine and amplify the meaning of the story. Banking off the enduring tension between Jews and Samaritans, the Johannine community declares that Jesus, the Word made flesh, transcends both modes of worship. The unusual occurrence of a lone woman encountering Jesus at the village well (note the shocked reaction of the disciples in 4:27) provides the setting for their encounter and a display of Jesus's prophetic knowledge about her life. The woman's testimony and the ultimate persuasion of the Samaritan villagers about Jesus's identity as the Messiah and the "Savior of the world" fits the Johannine pattern of discipleship and, at the same time, testifies to the early inclusion of Samaritans—consummate "outsiders" in the biblical history—as followers of Jesus. This latter fact prompted Raymond Brown and others to surmise that the early Johannine community had a significant representation of Samaritans, thus explaining the relative absence of Davidic (e.g., the "kingdom of God") motifs in John's Gospel and part of the reason for its unique characteristics compared to the Synoptic Gospels.[10]

JERUSALEM

Jerusalem and its environs, particularly the village of Bethany, which serves as a place of respite for Jesus, dominates the Johannine landscape. While in Jerusalem the Johannine Jesus further displays his divine identity and his mission of revealing the Father in both word and deed. Yet Jerusalem is also a zone of unrelenting hostility to Jesus. It begins with Jesus's going up to Jerusalem for the Passover and while there dramatically driving from the temple the sellers of animals and money-changers—both commercial enterprises needed for the sacrificial offerings (2:1–11).[11] Jesus's prophetic act leads to his declaration: "Destroy this temple and in three days I will raise it up." The narrator explains that Jesus was speaking about "the temple of his body" (2:13–22). Right from the start

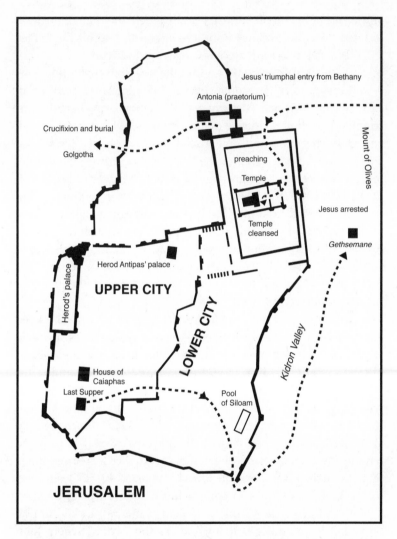

JERUSALEM

the overwhelming identity of Jesus's as the Word made flesh and the Son of God eclipses even the Jerusalem temple, long revered as the "house of God" and the focus of Jewish worship. In the Synoptic Gospels Jesus's prophetic cleansing of the temple comes at the end of his public ministry and triggers the final opposition to Jesus. John, too, relates Jesus's temple action to his death (see 2:22), but this powerful sign and reaction to it come at the very outset of his public ministry and set the tone for what follows.

Jesus goes to Jerusalem several times in John's account; in each instance his activities are a combination of powerful signs coupled with both evidence of faith by those who believe in him, and sharp rejection and polemic on the part of the "Jews."[12] In 5:1 he arrives for a "feast of the Jews." Since during the Gospel John will refer to the pilgrimage Feasts of Passover (2:13, 23; 6:4; 11:55; 12:1; 13:1; 18:28, 39; 19:14) and Tabernacles or Booths (7:2), this unidentified feast may be the third pilgrimage Feast of Pentecost. On this visit he will heal the paralyzed man at the pool of Bethesda (5:1–18), followed by the deadly reaction of his opponents who "tried all the more to kill him, because he not only broke the sabbath but he also called God his own father, making himself equal to God" (5:18).

In 7:10 Jesus again travels from Galilee to Jerusalem for the Feast of Tabernacles but in secret because his enemies in Judea were seeking to kill him (7:1). There follows an extended section of the Gospel (7:1 – 10:42), with Jesus fearlessly proclaiming his role as one sent by the Father and as the "light of the world," while his opponents seek, without success, to arrest him. Most of the action takes place in the temple area (7:14, 28, "in the temple area"; 8:20, "in the treasury in the temple area"; 8:59; 10:23, "in the temple area on the Portico of Solomon"). But the Gospel also notes that after a dispute among the Jewish leaders (7:40-52), Jesus goes to the Mount of Olives — perhaps implying a return to Bethany (7:53) — and again flees from his enemies' attempt to kill him by returning to the other Bethany "across the Jordan" where John had been baptizing.[13] Even here people come to him and "many there began to believe in him" (10:40-42).

During this visit to the Holy City, the ritual of the Feast of Tabernacles, a harvest feast in which Israel also prays for the coming of the winter rains, sets the stage for Jesus to declare he is the source of living water, which the narrator explains referred to the gift of the Spirit that Jesus would confer through his death and exaltation (7:37-39). The Gospel also notes the encounter of Jesus in the temple area with the woman caught in adultery (8:1-11),[14] the extended account of the healing of the man born blind at the pool of Siloam, and the revealing interaction among the man healed of blindness, his parents, the Jewish leaders, and Jesus himself (9:1-41). Jesus's discourse on the Good Shepherd (10:1-18) concludes with another round of debate with his opponents on the Feast of the Dedication (10:19-39), after which Jesus leaves Jerusalem for Bethany beyond the Jordan (10:40-42).

Preparation for the finale of the public ministry of Jesus begins with his going to Bethany after learning that Lazarus, the brother of Mary and Martha, and Jesus's own beloved friend (11:3, 35) has died. Again, John's Gospel characteristically blends discourse and narrative to proclaim Jesus's unique identity. Jesus declares, "I am the resurrection and the life," and at his command the dead Lazarus is freed from the tomb and restored to life (11:1-44). Commentators on John's Gospel have long understood that this scene represents both the summation of Jesus's mission — bringing life to the world out of love — and the transition point leading to the climax of the Gospel, Jesus's death and exaltation. The stir caused by the raising of Lazarus leads to the final deliberation of the Jewish religious leaders. The high priest Caiaphas declares that it was "better for you that one man should die instead of the people, so that the whole nation may not perish" (11:50). The narrator observes that unwittingly the high priest had prophesied "that Jesus was going to die for the nation, and not only for the nation, but also to gather into one the dispersed children of God" (11:51-52). The mounting hostility of the leaders and their determination to kill Jesus causes him to leave "for the region near the desert, to a town called Ephraim" (11:54).[15]

Jesus's climactic return to Jerusalem begins with a last visit to Bethany, where he is celebrated with a banquet with his friends Lazarus, Martha, and Mary (12:1–11). While Martha serves the meal, Mary anoints Jesus with costly perfumed oil, an act Jesus interprets as his burial anointing. The passion looms on the horizon, as the religious leaders determine to kill not only Jesus but also Lazarus (12:10–11). There follows Jesus's dramatic entry into Jerusalem (12:12–19), and then a request of "some Greeks" to see Jesus, an event that prompts Jesus to cry out in anguish, "I am troubled now" — what most commentators see as the Johannine version of the Gethsemane prayer found in the Synoptics. The unrelenting hostility of the religious authorities causes Jesus to hide from them, presumably somewhere in the Jerusalem area (12:36), although the Gospel does not identify the location.

THE FINALE

The Passion Narrative

The sequence of the Johannine passion narrative of chapters 18 – 19 and its general landscape have strong similarities with the Synoptic versions: the arrest of Jesus is followed by interrogation by the high priest and his colleagues, then transfer to a trial before Pilate, and finally crucifixion and burial. But here, too, John's distinctive perspective shines through. While the brutalities of the passion account remain, there is an underlying triumphant tone to John's passion.[16] The arresting party is overwhelmed by Jesus's presence; the disciples do not flee but are dismissed by Jesus; Jesus challenges the high priest and his attendants; Jesus mystifies and frightens Pilate; the crucifixion is portrayed as a coronation; Jesus speaks from the cross, creating a new community; from his open side flow blood and water, signs of salvation; he is buried in a new tomb and anointed as if a king. John's theology, which portrays Jesus's death as the completion of his mission to reveal

God's love for the world, has suffused his passion account with a spirit of exaltation, truly an "hour of glory."

After the conclusion of his final discourse, Jesus goes "across the Kidron valley to where there was a garden" where Jesus and his disciples "had often met" (18:1-2). John alone names the area as the "Kidron" (from the Hebrew word for "dark") valley east of Jerusalem and identifies it as a "garden," but the location coincides with Mark and Matthew's accounts, which refer to "Gethsemane" and with Luke, who identifies it as "the Mount of Olives" (22:39). Earlier in all three Synoptics, Jesus and his disciples had set out for the "Mount of Olives" at the conclusion of the Passover meal (Mark 14:26 et par.). There is no anguished prayer of Jesus at this point in John's account, since it was anticipated earlier (see 12:27-33).

After the arrest of Jesus, there follows the interrogation by the Jewish religious authorities. Only John's account has Jesus taken first to the "courtyard" of Annas, "the father-in-law of Caiaphas," the reigning high priest (18:12-15), and later brought to Caiaphas himself (18:24). John alone adds the curious incident of Peter at first standing outside "at the gate" and then being brought inside by "the other disciple, the acquaintance of the high priest" (18:15-16). This sets the stage for Peter's denials when confronted by "the maid who was the gatekeeper," as well as noting the presence within the passion account of one who presumably is the "Beloved Disciple" (see 13:23-26).

After Jesus is brought to Caiaphas (John offers no details about this meeting), he is then taken to Pilate, a scene of great importance in John's account. John identifies the location as the "praetorium," a Roman military term that came to mean the residence or headquarters of a commander (see also Mark 15:16; Matt 27:27). John's unique staging of the scene has the Jewish leaders standing outside (not wanting to incur ritual defilement by entering the Gentile abode, so that they could "eat the Passover," 18:28) and Pilate shuttling back and forth from inside the praetorium to question Jesus and then back outside where he jousts with the leaders. As Pilate's apprehension about the mysterious identity of Jesus grows (see 19:8–12), in a final attempt to free Jesus, he has him scourged and brought out wearing a crown of thorns and a purple cloak—mock symbols of royalty—and presents him to the crowd, "Behold, the man." In the face of the crowd's rejection of Jesus, Pilate even seems to place Jesus on the judgment seat, a place that John describes in detail as a "place called Stone Pavement, in Hebrew, Gabbatha" (19:13)—capping a series of ironic gestures.[17] While the crowds and Pilate—each for different motives— mock Jesus's pretensions to kingship, the reader of the Gospel knows that, in fact, Jesus is a king like no other. After the rejection by the crowd prevails, Jesus is brought to the place of execution that John identifies as "the Place of the Skull, in Hebrew, Golgotha," a designation agreed to by all four Gospels.

Following Jesus's dramatic death ("It is finished," 19:30) and the signs that accompany it—the bones of the "Lamb of God" not broken and the flow of blood and water from Jesus's pierced side—John recounts the burial of Jesus. Joseph of Arimathea, also mentioned in the Synoptics, claims the body of Jesus from Pilate, and is joined in John's account by Nicodemus, the Jewish leader who had encountered Jesus in the first discourse of the Gospel (3:1–21) and later defended Jesus (7:50–52). Nicodemus had first come to Jesus "by night" (3:2; 19:39) but now is described as bringing an enormous amount of myrrh and aloes to anoint the body of Jesus in a manner fit for a king. Joseph and Nicodemus, in some ways the first to be drawn to Jesus in the wake of his death, place him in a "new tomb" in a "garden" in the place where he had been crucified. John's identification of the burial place in a "garden" anticipates the resurrection appearance stories of chapter 20 and may evoke memory of the Garden of Eden and the new creation brought about by Jesus's redemptive death.[18]

RESURRECTION APPEARANCES IN JERUSALEM

Here again John's unique perspective is evident. As in the Synoptics, there is a discovery of the empty tomb on the "first day of the week," but John introduces the significant role of Mary Magdalene. She comes to the tomb alone (20:1) and finding it empty, runs to alert Simon Peter and the Beloved Disciple, assuming that someone has taken Jesus's body from the tomb. Simon Peter and the Beloved Disciple run to the tomb, with the Beloved Disciple arriving first and waiting for Peter to get there.[19] They observe the burial cloth and the cloth that covered Jesus's head carefully folded and laid aside, but their response is not yet complete. They return to their homes, the Gospel notes, but Mary remains outside the tomb weeping (20:10–11). It is Mary Magdalene who, in the following beautiful scene at the garden, will encounter Christ and finally realize that he is risen from the dead (20:11–18); she is the one who will announce the resurrection to the rest of the disciples (20:18), echoing once more the Johannine motif of an encounter with Christ leading to testimony (see the response of the first disciples and of the Samaritan woman).

Two more encounters with the risen Christ conclude the resurrection appearances in Jerusalem—each unique to John's Gospel. John locates the encounters in a place where "the doors were locked...for fear of the Jews" but adds no further details. Both are presumably in Jerusalem, with the first happening the evening of the same day that Jesus had appeared to Mary (20:19). Here again John's Gospel shrouds Jerusalem with a sense of threat, as experienced by Jesus during his lifetime and now by the disciples in the wake of his crucifixion. But the appearance of the crucified (his wounds are visible) and risen Christ brings to his disciples "rejoicing," "peace," and the power of the Spirit, which will guide them in the mission now entrusted to them (see 20:19–23). John recounts a second appearance "a week later" (20:26), also in a place with locked doors, this time for the sake of Thomas. His

117

demand to touch Jesus's wounds as the condition for belief gives way to perhaps the most explicit confession of Jesus's identity in the Gospel: "My Lord and my God" (20:28).

SUMMATION

Jerusalem plays a major role in John's portrayal of the mission of Jesus, with his repeated visits, multiple signs and discourses, and sharply polemical interactions with his opponents. Along with his knowledge of Jewish festivals, John's Gospel also displays a significant awareness of the topography of Jerusalem. In addition to places cited in the Synoptics such as the Mount of Olives, Bethany (but playing a much larger role in John's account), the temple area, the Roman praetorium, and Golgotha, John's account also knows about the Sheep's Gate and the five porticoed pools of Bethesda (5:1), the pool of Siloam (9:7), and specific names such as the Kidron Valley (18:1) and "Gabbatha" (19:13). In speaking of the temple area, John also specifies the "Portico of Solomon" and the "treasury." John also refers to villages in the surrounding region such as "Bethany across the Jordan," "Aonem near Salim, and "Ephraim." The Fourth Gospel musters all this information as the significant backdrop for the mission of Jesus.

AT THE SEA OF TIBERIAS

John's Gospel concludes with a resurrection appearance of Jesus to some of his disciples at the Sea of Galilee. Since the evangelist seems to bring his narrative to a formal close at the end of chapter 20 (see 20:20–31), many commentators consider chapter 21 as a kind of "appendix" added to the Gospel, although there is no extent manuscript of the Fourth Gospel with this chapter missing. The appearance is one of the New Testament's most exquisite narratives. John locates the scene "at the Sea of Tiberias" (21:1) – a designation for the sea already noted in 6:1. The first part of the story describes Peter, along with Thomas and Nathanael, who were previously mentioned in the Gospel, now joined by "Zebedee's sons" and two other unnamed disciples, going fishing. Unlike the Synoptics, where Jesus's first disciples (Simon, Andrew, and Zebedee's sons James and John) are fishermen and Jesus's words use the metaphor of fishing to characterize their future mission of "catching men" (see also Luke 5:1–11), John does not use such language nor, as we have seen, does John accentuate the role of the sea in his narrative compared to the Synoptics.[20] Similar to Luke's account of the call of Simon, which includes a miraculous catch (Luke 5:6, 9), so here, Jesus's instructions lead to a great catch of "one hundred fifty-three large fish" — a precise number whose significance has forever baffled interpreters.

In the sequence of events that will follow, the Johannine Jesus turns to the more familiar metaphor of caring for the sheep. In a scene without parallel in all the Gospels, the risen Jesus prepares breakfast for his amazed disciples, and at the conclusion of the meal heals Peter's threefold denial (see 18:15–17) by drawing from him a threefold confession of his love for Jesus. In turn Jesus commissions him to "feed my sheep" (21:15–19). The scene ends with Jesus's prediction of Peter's martyrdom and a final word about the destiny of the Beloved Disciple (21:21–23). This reference to the Beloved Disciple ushers in his final testimony that concludes John's Gospel: "There are also many other things that Jesus did, but if these were to be described individually, I do not think the whole world would contain the books that would be written" (21:25).

CONCLUSION

Tracing the landscape of the Gospel of John vividly illustrates the important role of geography and its historical overlay in proclaiming the evangelist's message. The Fourth Gospel uniquely envelops the life and mission of Jesus in a "spatial" or cosmic dimension that tracks the origin of the Word within the very heart of God. The Word made flesh definitively reveals God and God's intent to save the world. His mission accomplished in the unimpeachable love expressed through laying down his life on the cross, the Word returns to the Father, sending the Spirit to enliven his disciples and to embolden them to proclaim God's Word to the world, and so to complete the divine plan for human destiny that "all may be one."

The Word made flesh, Jesus of Nazareth, carries out his earthly mission in word and deed (i.e., "signs") in the arena of first-century Palestine. For John's Gospel—distinct from the narrative framework of the Synoptics—the fateful arena of Jesus's mission is focused on Jerusalem more than on Galilee. Here is where Jesus will complete his mission of revealing God's love for the world, and here the crucified and risen Christ will appear to Mary Magdalene and his disciples and gift them with the Holy Spirit and with the mission entrusted to him by his Father. A final interlude in Galilee closes the narrative, with the risen Christ serving his disciples breakfast and restoring Peter to his pastoral leadership.

CONCLUSION

Seeking the Holy Land

Tracking the landscape of the Gospels and the Acts of the Apostles reminds us that the incarnation is central to Christian faith. We dare to believe that the "Word became flesh." In Jesus of Nazareth, a first-century Jew, the presence of the eternal and transcendent God was embodied and dwelt among us. Because Jesus was human, he lived in a particular time and place. Because he was divine, the land he touched was and is sacred.

The Gospels and Acts confirm this for us. Our study has shone in detail that their portrayal of Jesus and the early Christian mission carried out in his name was not abstract. The life of Jesus was not timeless or landless. Jesus lived in the first third of the first century, under the rule of Herod Antipas in Lower Galilee and direct Roman occupation in Judea and Samaria. The mission of Jesus was carried out in the fishing village of Capernaum and in Solomon's Portico of the Jerusalem temple. He preached in first-century synagogues and sailed across the Sea of Galilee and moved through the villages and towns of the region. He stayed with friends in Bethany and was crucified on Golgotha outside the city gates of Jerusalem. And when Luke describes the post-Easter Christian mission, it begins in Jerusalem and then breaks out into the Mediterranean world: Antioch, Ephesus, Thessalonica, Rome, and many places in between.

Christians, therefore, venerate the Holy Land because God's people were formed there and, most of all, because Jesus lived there. The Church over time locates shrines or holy places

121

to commemorate incidents in the Gospels: the Basilica of the Nativity in Bethlehem, the Basilica of the Annunciation in Nazareth, the entire remains of the village of Capernaum, the shrine of the Transfiguration on Mount Tabor, the Church of All Nations in Gethsemane, the Holy Sepulchre in Jerusalem, and so on. So, too, throughout the Mediterranean world, churches and shrines remember Paul and the apostles: in Philippi and Athens, in Ephesus and Antioch, in Malta and Rome. From the earliest centuries, Christians have traveled—often at their peril—on pilgrimage to such holy places and brought back vials of oil or bits of earth and stone from these lands as a remembrance. Great scholars like Jerome in the fourth century moved from Rome to Bethlehem, to learn the language of the Scriptures, to get the lay of the land, and to study and translate the Bible. Generations of pilgrims and scholars would follow until this very day.

Yet with all this sacredness of the biblical lands and Christian veneration of them, Catholic Christian faith makes no ultimate territorial claims on the historic land of Israel. The destiny of God's people, in the eyes of Christian faith, is not a return to the physical boundaries of the Holy Land where Jesus lived. A baptism of a child in Capetown, South Africa; or Bogota, Columbia; or Chicago, Illinois, is no less valid or sacred than a baptism enacted at the venerable baptismal site at the Jordan River. Christ is no less present in Paris, France, or Bangalore, India, than in Nazareth, Israel. For Christians, God's promises to Israel, including the gift of the land, finds its ultimate fulfillment and embodiment in the person of Jesus Christ. Jesus, crucified and risen, and abiding among God's people—that is the true "holy land." Following Jesus and living in his Spirit can take place anywhere on this earth and there is no land or space from which that presence can be excluded.

As we have seen, this movement beyond the land of Israel is already present in the Gospels and the Acts of the Apostles. The Gentile who had lived among the tombs is healed and sent off to proclaim the gospel message in the Decapolis. The amazing faith of a centurion in Capernaum inspires Jesus to see many coming from the nations east and west to join Abraham's table. Jesus stands in the Jerusalem temple and declares that his own body will be the locus of God's presence. In a room in Jerusalem, the risen Jesus sends his disciples to go to "the ends of the earth." On a mountaintop in Galilee, the same risen Christ commissions his disciples to go to "all nations" and promises to be "with them until the end of time." A storm of the Spirit falls upon the disciples huddled in fear in Jerusalem, and impelled by that Spirit, their preaching is understood by all. On the road to Damascus, an appearance of the risen Christ will channel the excessive zeal of Paul into his tireless mission to the Gentiles. In the words of the risen Christ in the Acts of the Apostles, God's salvation begins "in Jerusalem" but then moves out to "Judea and Samaria, and the ends of the earth" (Acts 1:8).

In fact, in the New Testament writings in general, we see this transformation from the particularities of the incarnation to its universal yet still embodied presence. Thus, the temple is no longer confined to Jerusalem (although the earliest followers of Jesus worshiped there) but is understood as the "body" of Christ (John 2:21), as the Church itself (Eph 2:19–22), and even as the individual Christian in whom the Spirit of God dwells (1 Cor 3:16–17; 6:19; 2 Cor 6:16). "Jerusalem" remains a holy city within the boundaries of the Holy Land, but Christians also long for a "new Jerusalem" that will be a transformed dwelling place for the children of God that is beautiful and secure and filled with God's presence (Rev 21:2–4).

Squaring Catholic convictions about the Holy Land with modern Jewish perspectives on the land can be challenging. Taking modern Catholic teaching as a guide, we as Christians respect Judaism's distinctive view of the land of Israel as God's gift to the Jewish people. The modern State of Israel is essentially a secular state, but that does not rob it of its unique significance for Jewish tradition and observant Jewish faith. Saint Pope John Paul II had a profound reverence for Jews and was the first pope to establish diplomatic relations between the Vatican and the State of Israel. On many fronts, particularly since the Second Vatican Council, the Roman Catholic Church has sought to heal the wounds of the past inflicted by Christian anti-Semitism, and to draw closer to the Jewish community. Part of the task of developing mutual understanding on the part of Catholics is to appreciate the meaning of Israel for Jews, even for those who live in the Diaspora and will never live in present-day Israel.

Catholic teaching also affirms that the land is a gift of God, not an unconditional possession. This, too, is Jewish and biblical tradition. God gives a land of promise to his people but also requires their continuing obedience to the law, including respect for the "the widow, the orphan, and the sojourner." While some Old Testament traditions imply the land is to be taken as a conquest, other biblical traditions remind the people of their own experience of slavery and counsel a spirit of justice and compassion for all. In the Gospels, Jesus is portrayed as reverencing Jerusalem and its temple, and, especially in the Gospel of Matthew, is conscious of the unique status of Israel ("Go rather to the lost sheep of the house of Israel," Matt 10:5). Yet the Jesus of the Gospels emphatically reaches out to those on the margins and defends those who are considered "sinners" and "outside the law." Thus Catholic teaching both reverences current Israel as the locus (along with the surrounding regions of Palestine, Jordan, Lebanon, and Egypt) of so many biblical and gospel events, but also urges respect for the rights of Palestinians and other non-Jews in the region. The Catholic Church, in conjunction with other Christian groups, has also urged respect for the rights of the local Christians of the Holy Land, and for continuing access to the holy sites for pilgrims who come from all over the world.

The biblical landscape remains sacred for us as Christians, and those who wish a deeper knowledge of the Scriptures should not forget the actual historical world in which the Scriptures were formed. While most Christians will not have the opportunity to travel to the Holy Land and see the holy sites firsthand, modern print and visual media has made a virtual exploration of these sacred places more accessible than at any time in Christian history. Especially for those who want to study the Scriptures in a formal way and perhaps to teach the Bible or lead Bible study groups, becoming more familiar with the biblical landscape can only enhance our knowledge and love of the Scriptures.

When all is said and done regarding the biblical landscape, the essential reality is that the infinitely transcendent God created the world out of love and made humans, male and female, in the divine image. We are both of the earth and of God. Thus, every land is a sacred arena and a place where we are called to dwell in peace and justice together. The historical presence of God's people Israel and his Son Jesus in a particular land and at a particular time confirms for every place and all times our human dignity and our eternal destiny.

Notes

INTRODUCTION

1. The account of Israel's history described in the Bible, particularly in the long stretch of time and events covered in the Old Testament, should not be understood in an overly literal way. No doubt, theological perspectives and literary creativity have left their mark on the biblical narrative. Nevertheless, there are both historical and geographical realities entwined within the biblical account and its landscape. On this see Donald Senior, *Composing Sacred Scripture: How the Bible Was Formed* (Chicago: LTP, 2017).

2. Obviously the landscape of the Acts of the Apostles opens a different geographical and historical vista than the traditional arena of biblical history; see below, pp. 76–96.

3. Roman presence in the Middle East began in 63 BC, when they were invited in during a period of great civil unrest. Herod the Great was established as a vassal king under the domination of Roman power in 47 BC.

4. See Jordan J. Ryan, *The Role of the Synagogue in the Aims of Jesus* (Minneapolis: Fortress Press, 2017); also, Lidia D. Matassa, *Invention of the First-Century Synagogue* (Atlanta: SBL Press, 2018).

5. Bet Shean is the only city of the Decapolis to be located on the western side of the Jordan River.

6. On the landscape of the Gospel of John, see below, pp. 97–120.

7. See below, pp. 76–95.

CHAPTER ONE

1. See above, pp. 17–19.

2. The biblical portrayal of the exodus is a prime example of how the Bible's historical narrative cannot be taken simply as a literal historical account. What is presented as a singular, decisive, and dramatic event in the Bible may represent a much more complex and extended period of historical migration of Semitic peoples into the land of Canaan. The Gospel writers such as Mark take the biblical account at face value. See above, introduction, pp. 3–5.

3. On the general landscape and historical background of Galilee, see above, pp. 8–13.

4. On the Sea of Galilee, see above, pp. 13–14.

5. See Elizabeth McNamer, *The Case for Bethsaida after Twenty Years of Digging: Understanding the Historical Jesus* (Cambridge: Cambridge Scholars Publishing, 2017).

6. On the Decapolis, see above, pp. 10–11.

7. See below, pp. 49–50, 53–56.

8. However, from the sixth century onward, except for the brief Hasmonean dynasty, the Jews did not have political control of their own land but were successively under the Babylonian, Persian, Greek, and Roman Empires. On Jerusalem, see above, pp. 19–20.

9. The religious leaders in John 2:20 claim that the temple had been under construction for "forty-six years," a statement that would have been fairly accurate during the lifetime of Jesus.

10. See Donald Senior, *Why the Cross?* (Nashville: Abingdon Press, 2016), 1–9.

CHAPTER TWO

1. The Sermon on the Mount, chs. 5–7; the Mission Discourse, ch. 10; the Parable Discourse, ch. 13; the Community Discourse, ch. 18; and the Apocalyptic Discourse, chs. 24–25.

2. See above, pp. 5–7.

3. See above, pp. 10–12.

4. See Donald Senior, *The Passion of Jesus in the Gospel of Matthew* (Wilmington, DE: Michael Glazier, 1985).

CHAPTER THREE

1. Luke uses the first-person plural in Acts 16:10–18; 20:4 – 21:9; 27:1 – 28:30.

2. See above, pp. 11–12.

3. See pp. 14–17; see also the role of Samaria in the Gospel of John, pp. 107–110.

4. For the nuances of Luke's passion narrative, see D. Senior, *The Passion of Jesus in the Gospel of Luke* (Wilmington, DE: Michael Glazier, 1989).

5. The precise location of Emmaus is debated, and the distance from Jerusalem cited by Luke varies in some ancient manuscripts.

6. On the mission to Samaria described in Acts, see above, p. 79.

7. On the role of geography in this key episode, see Benjamin R. Wilson, "Jew-Gentile Relations and the Geographic Movement of Acts 10:1 – 11:18," *CBQ* 80 (2018): 81–96.

8. Under the Seleucid dynasty (312–63 BC), several cities in Asia Minor were named after the Seleucid ruler Antiochus. The major city of Antioch on the Orontes River is referred to here as the base for Paul and Barnabas. Their missionary travels will take them to another "Antioch" of Pisidia (see Acts 13:14).

9. Because Acts will focus on the mission of Paul to the west, the equally important development of Christianity to the east is overlooked, with the exception of Paul's brief sojourn in Damascus. Christians living in modern regions such as Syria and Iraq and as far east as India also trace their origins to apostolic times.

10. Originally a Macedonian city, it was named after Philip II. Later after 42 BC, it became a Roman colony, heavily populated by army veterans.

11. Lydia is identified as a native of Thyatira in present-day western Turkey. Purple dye was very expensive to manufacture, and it is likely that Lydia was a prosperous businesswoman who apparently also owned her own home.

12. Most smaller ships would hug the coast during the day, staying overnight at an anchorage or a small harbor.

13. The games were held in AD 51, prompting some historians to suggest that this was the reason Paul traveled to Corinth to take advantage of this opportunity for evangelization.

14. A fragment of an inscription found at Delphi refers to Gallio's tenure dating from the latter half of AD 51, thus providing a reference point for the date of Paul's stay in Corinth.

CHAPTER FOUR

1. Recent scholarship has emphasized the Jewish provenance of John's Gospel, particularly since the discovery of the Dead Sea Scrolls has revealed certain literary and theological perspectives not unlike those found in the Fourth Gospel.

2. John distinguishes between creation (literally, "all things," *panta re*) and the "world" (*kosmos*); the latter includes humanity itself and is capable of both accepting and rejecting the Word (John 1:10–13).

3. The term "glory" (*doxa*) is used in the Greek Septuagint to translate the Hebrew *kabod Yahweh*, i.e., the manifest presence (literally, the "heaviness") of the divine.

4. The Madaba map is found on a mosaic floor of a sixth-century AD church and portrays with remarkable accuracy the location of numerous biblical sites in the Holy Land.

5. Note especially the alternations made by Matthew's Gospel in Matt 4:12–17; see above, pp. 54–55.

6. Jesus moves to Galilee in 1:43; returns to Jerusalem in 2:13; returns to Galilee by way of Samaria in 4:3, 43; returns to Jerusalem in 5:1; back to Galilee in 6:1 (an abrupt transition); goes back to Jerusalem in secret in 7:10. In 10:40 Jesus flees Jerusalem to go to Bethany beyond the Jordan and returns to Bethany and Jerusalem in 11:7 upon hearing of Lazarus's death. In 11:54 Jesus again flees Jerusalem for the Judean village of Ephraim and returns to Jerusalem in 12:1. In 12:36, John notes that Jesus "hides" from the leaders but does not indicate where.

7. The present-day location of Cana in Kifr Kana near Nazareth is not the historical location of first-century Cana, which is probably identified with Kirbet Kana, a site also in Lower Galilee.

8. Some interpreters consider this evidence that John knew the Synoptic Gospels or, at least, the pre-gospel traditions of John and the Synoptics had some cross-fertilization.

9. Some commentators consider her coming to the well alone as indicative of her outlying status in the village, perhaps because of her unusual marriage record. The well in Middle Eastern territory traditionally is the place where women gather not only to draw water but to share news and gossip.

10. Note that in this regard both John's Gospel and the Acts of the Apostles testify to the early inclusion of Samaritans as followers of Jesus. See R. Brown, *Community of the Beloved Disciple* (New York: Paulist Press, 1979), 35–40.

11. Only special coins minted in Lebanon without any Roman inscriptions or images were permitted as offerings in the temple; thus the need for money-changers.

12. In John's Gospel, the term "Jews" in most instances refers to Jews who did not believe in Jesus; in fact, however, Jesus's own early followers were themselves Jews.

13. See above, pp. 101–2.

14. Many commentators believe that this may not have been part of the original Johannine narrative. It is missing in many early Greek manuscripts.

15. This may be the modern town of et-Taiyebeh, located north of Jerusalem on a high point not far from Jericho and its desert region. Eusebius refers to a village in this location named "Ephrem" in his *Onomasticon* (s.v. "Afra"). Villagers there today identify their town as the place where Jesus took refuge.

16. See D. Senior, *The Passion of Jesus in the Gospel of John* (Collegeville, MN: Liturgical Press, 1991).

17. John's text combines a series of words here to describe the place where Pilate seats Jesus. The Greek word *bema* (translated in the NABRE as "judgment seat") refers to an elevated platform found in public places such as a forum where judicial decisions or other matters were determined; *lithostrotos* means literally a "stone pavement"; and the Hebrew word *Gabbatha* also refers to an elevated place.

18. Note that John's unique description of the location of Jesus burial ("in the place where he had been crucified") also coincides with the strong tradition (bolstered by archaeology) that locates the place of both the crucifixion and the tomb of Jesus at the present-day Church of the Holy Sepulchre.

19. As in other places in John's account, there is deference for Peter (see 6:66-69), but the Fourth Gospel clearly considers the Beloved Disciple to have a singular relationship with Jesus and the meaning of his mission: see, e.g., the Beloved Disciple's presence at the cross 19:25-27 and his testimony about the truth of the Gospel (19:35; 21:24-25).

20. See above, pp. 105-7.

Select Bibliography

Aharoni, Yohanan. *The Land of the Bible: A Historical Geography*, rev. ed. Philadelphia: Westminster Press, 1979. A classic detailed study of the history and geography of ancient Israel.

Bruggemann, Walter. *The Land*. Overtures to Biblical Theology. Philadelphia: Fortress Press, 1977. A now-classic study of the meaning of the "land" from an Old Testament perspective.

Burge, Gary M. *Jesus and the Land: The New Testament Challenge to "Holy Land" Theology*. Grand Rapids: Baker Academic, 2010. A thoughtful challenge to what the author sees as a dangerous overemphasis on theological claims of some Christians regarding the State of Israel.

Chancey, Mark A. *Greco-Roman Culture and the Galilee of Jesus*. SNTS MS 134. Cambridge University Press, 2005. Emphasizes the Jewish character of Galilee at the time of Jesus.

Davies, W. D. *The Gospel and the Land: Early Christianity and Jewish Territorial Doctrine*. Berkeley: University of California Press, 1974. A historical and exegetical study of the theological meaning of the land from a mainly New Testament perspective.

Hanson, K. C., and Douglas E. Oakman. *Palestine in the Time of Jesus: Social Structures and Social Conflicts*. 2nd ed. Minneapolis: Fortress Press, 2008. Reviews the social, political, and economic context of Palestine in the early first century.

Keener, Craig S. *Acts: An Exegetical Commentary*. 4 vols. Grand Rapids: Baker Academic, 2012–15. A massive commentary on the Acts of the Apostles that considers all aspects of this key New Testament text, including the social and political context of the regions covered by the narrative of Acts.

Matassa, Lidia D. *Invention of the First-Century Synagogue*. Atlanta: SBL Press, 2018. The author argues that the material evidence does not support a distinctive architecture for synagogues in Palestine until beyond the first century.

McNamer, Elizabeth. *The Case for Bethsaida after Twenty Years of Digging*. Newcastle upon Tyne: Cambridge Scholars Publishing, 2017. A testimonial by one who has been involved in the archaeological dig at Bethsaida.

Niehoff, Maren R., ed. *Journeys in the Roman East: Imagined and Real*. Tübingen: Mohr Siebeck, 2017. The development of Roman roads and their relative safety led to an explosion of travel and travel accounts in the first century, reflected as well in the Acts of the Apostles.

Notley, R. Steven. *In the Master's Steps: The Gospels in the Land*. Jerusalem: Carta Jerusalem, 2014. Beautifully illustrated survey of the land and settlements of Palestine at the time of Jesus.

Pixner, Bargil. *With Jesus through Galilee according to the Fifth Gospel*. Rosh Pina, Israel: Corazim Publishing, 1992. A labor of love from a working archaeologist and Benedictine monk living in Galilee that tracks the Gospel accounts in relation to present-day Galilee.

Pritchard, James, and Nick Page, eds. *Harper Collins Atlas of Bible History*. New York: Harper Collins, 2009. Provides maps and commentary on the history and geography of the Bible, both Old and New Testaments.

Reed, Jonathan L. *Archaeology and the Galilean Jesus: A Re-examination of the Evidence*. Harrisburg, PA: Trinity Press International, 2000. A fine summation of how modern archaeology has informed our knowledge of Galilee at the time of Jesus.

Romey, Kristin. "The Search for the Real Jesus." *National Geographic*. December 2017, 54–69. A superbly illustrated and reliable summation of the archaeology and geography related to the Jesus of history, with special emphasis on the church of the Holy Sepulchre and its recent renovations.

Ryan, Jordan J. *The Role of the Synagogue in the Aims of Jesus.* Minneapolis: Fortress Press, 2017. Emphasizes the important role of the synagogue in village life at the time of Jesus.

Thurston, Bonnie B. *The Spiritual Landscape of Mark.* Collegeville, MN: Liturgical Press, 1989. A rich spiritual reflection on the landscape of Mark's Gospel.

Verheyden, Joseph, and John S. Kloppenborg, eds. *Luke on Jesus, Paul and Christianity: What Did He Really Know?* Leuven: Peeters, 2017. A series of essays probing the reliability and sources of Luke's portrayal of Paul's mission in Acts.

Walton, Steve, Paul R. Trebilco, and David W. J. Gill, eds. *The Urban World and the First Christians.* Grand Rapids: Eerdmans, 2017. A series of essays exploring the urban context encountered by Paul and other early Christian missionaries.